pretty in patchwork

doll quilts

24 LITTLE QUILTS TO PIECE, STITCH, AND LOVE

cathy gaubert

LARK
CRAFTS

An Imprint of Sterling Publishing Co., Inc.
New York

WWW.LARKCRAFTS.COM

Editor: Amanda Carestio

Assistant Editor: Thom O'Hearn

Copyeditor: Nancy Wood

Art Directors: Megan Kirby, Amy Sly

Junior Designer: Meagan Shirlen

Illustrators: Orrin Lundgren (stitches
and templates), Aimee Ray (how-to)

Photographers: Susan Wasinger,
Lynne Harty, Steve Mann,
Jessica VanDerMark

Cover Designer: Amy Sly

Dedication:
*To my grandmothers, Edwina
and Florence, and to my mom…
for sharing with me the wonders
of needle and thread (and yarn).*

Library of Congress Cataloging-in-Publication Data

Gaubert, Cathy.
  Pretty in patchwork : doll quilts : 24 little quilts to piece, stitch, and love /
Cathy Gaubert. -- 1st ed.
    p. cm.
  Includes index.
  ISBN 978-1-60059-924-8
  1. Patchwork--Patterns. 2. Quilting--Patterns. 3. Doll quilts. 4. Miniature
quilts. I. Title.
  TT835.G33172 2011
  746.46'041--dc22

                                        2011008118

10 9 8 7 6 5 4 3 2 1

First Edition

Published by Lark Crafts
An Imprint of Sterling Publishing Co., Inc.
387 Park Avenue South, New York, NY 10016

Text © 2011, Cathy Gaubert
Photography © 2011, Lark Crafts, an Imprint of Sterling Publishing Co., Inc.,
unless otherwise specified
Illustrations © 2011, Lark Crafts, an Imprint of Sterling Publishing Co., Inc.,
unless otherwise specified

Distributed in Canada by Sterling Publishing,
c/o Canadian Manda Group, 165 Dufferin Street
Toronto, Ontario, Canada M6K 3H6

Distributed in the United Kingdom by GMC Distribution Services,
Castle Place, 166 High Street, Lewes, East Sussex, England BN7 1XU

Distributed in Australia by Capricorn Link (Australia) Pty Ltd.,
P.O. Box 704, Windsor, NSW 2756 Australia

If you have questions or comments about this book, please contact:
Lark Crafts
67 Broadway
Asheville, NC 28801
828-253-0467

Manufactured in China

ISBN 13: 978-1-60059-924-8

For information about custom editions, special sales, premium and corporate
purchases, please contact Sterling Special Sales Department at 800-805-5489 or
specialsales@sterlingpub.com.

For information about desk and examination copies available to college and
university professors, requests must be submitted to academic@larkbooks.com.
Our complete policy can be found at www.larkcrafts.com.

table of contents

welcome

Why, hello there! If you're holding this little book in your hands, then you, my friend, are in for a triple dose of awesomeness. From fabulous designers to yummy fabrics to pretty patchwork, you'll find 24 little reasons to make your heart happy.

Truly, the doll quilt is the perfect package. You can stitch up one of these lovelies in next to no time at all. What was once a rite of passage for young girls as they practiced their sewing skills is now the darling of the quilting world, especially for busy people—like myself—who dream of king-sized quilts that they'll never have time to make. With doll quilts, you can try a new technique, pour some stitched goodness into it, and forget about making any major commitment.

Heaps of scrap-busting potential? Check. Quilting techniques that will challenge you? Check. Helpful illustrations, shortcuts and snippets, and detailed instructions for creating dreamy doll quilts? But, of course. And new takes on traditional blocks? Absolutely! You'll find some of the standards—Dresden plates, maverick stars, and spiderwebs, all spruced up and fresh—and you're bound to find some new faves, like diamonds, plus signs, and hexagons. Really, you won't be able to make just one. Doll quilts are sort of like bunnies…the cuteness multiplies with each creation. And sometimes they're exactly like bunnies: take a peek at Andrea Zuill's Dancing Rabbit doll quilt on page 104.

Follow our instructions to the letter, or let the spirit of the quilt inspire your own inventive design. The projects range from perfectly pieced—check out Jacob's Ladder on page 94—to wonderfully wonky—like the Crazy Quilt on page 44—and everything in between. Experiment. Improvise. Those bits and pieces of fabric near your sewing machine are begging to be stitched up!

Cathy Gaubert

"It's who you are and what you do and how you make it…and that's why it's perfect."

My five-year-old daughter, Eme

Welcome to Pretty in Patchwork, a fresh new series that explores the sweet spot where sewing and quilting come together. Doll Quilts are the perfect starting place for patchwork fun... Stay tuned to see where we're headed next!

the basics

Okay, I know why you're here: for the quilties, of course! All of these quilts involve a bit of patchwork, including some improv piecing, but it's good to have a solid grounding in the techniques before you haul off and wing it. So if you need a refresher first—a few handy tips about piecing, quilting, binding, and all kinds of other fun along the way—here goes!

hello, dolly!

You'll notice this little handmade dolly, a cute dinosaur, and two sweet bunnies making appearances throughout this book. What's a doll quilt book without dolls anyway? Visit www.LarkCrafts.com/Bonus for instructions on how to make your own.

the materials

My guess is you probably don't need much assistance in gathering up your goods, especially if you're the type who regularly enjoys "quality time" in your local quilt shop. Doll quilts are so much fun in this regard; you don't need a whole lot of anything to make a masterpiece.

fabric

There is just so much good fabric to be found that sometimes it can make your head spin (in a totally good way, that is). I'm quite sure that you have a nice little (or big? who am I kidding…of course it's big!) stash to gaze at lovingly. However, don't overlook those linen maternity pants, that super-cute floral skirt that has gotten a wee bit too tight, or your sweet babe's outgrown goodies when you're on the hunt for fabric supplies. Repurposing fabric is not only good for the Earth and the soul, but also for the pocketbook—not to mention the charm and nostalgia your little quilty will inspire. A trip to the thrift shop or a tag sale can yield lovely wool garments begging to be cut up, along with vintage linens just waiting to be reborn. I always wash these cotton fabric finds before using them, but I'll admit that I rarely wash the quilting cottons I buy. I tell myself that it's because I love to pull a warm, yummy, crinkly quilt from the dryer, and this is most definitely true. However, I also know I'm not nearly organized enough to wash, press, and fold the yards of new fabrics that come to live in my home. So, there is my little secret. If you are at all concerned about the fabric's color fastness or the shrinkage factor, then by all means wash and press and fold away (it's better to be safe than sorry).

threads & embroidery floss

A quick word about threads: Cotton-poly blends are my favorite. They're readily available and they come in so many glorious colors. Be sure to have an assortment on hand to match to your fabrics. If you plan to machine-quilt your piece, you'll want to use a thread made for that purpose. For hand-quilting, nothing makes me happier than picking my way through skeins of colorful embroidery floss until I find the perfect shade to blend with (or boldly accent) my quilt top.

batting

Everyone has a favorite batting (or wadding), and the most popular ones are either 100% cotton, 100% polyester, or a poly blend. For the doll quilts in this book, 100% cotton is the standard. Of course, you can always repurpose some flannel, hunt down some wool, or go green with bamboo batting. Whatever you choose, you won't need very much of it for these little quilties.

fusible webbing & adhesives

A few projects will have you extolling the virtues of fusible web. It's a quick and painless way to adhere fabrics for easy appliquéing. A bottle of fray-check and a washable glue stick will come in handy as well.

the tools

One of the wonderful things about quilting is that you can create all kinds of awesome with the most basic of toolkits. Really, you can totally kick it old school with just a needle, thread, and scissors. Of course, there's no reason to eschew technology, so feel free to get as geared up as you want; I know I'm not leaving my walking foot up on a shelf!

basic patchwork kit

- sewing machine
- rotary cutting system (cutter + mat + assortment of quilting rulers)
- scissors (sewing + craft)
- straight + quilter's pins
- hand-sewing needles
- ironing board + iron (steam is your friend, but watch those fingertips!)
- embroidery kit (needles, hoops, water soluble pen, floss, and transfer tools)
- pencil
- seam ripper
- thread
- quilting/masking tape or spray basting adhesive

putting it all together

While some projects call for a healthy dose of perfection, others encourage you to relax the rules a bit with impromptu piecing. Here, there, or somewhere in-between, patchwork is the unifying theme. Peruse the projects and your stash, and let your whimsy be your guide!

templates

Turn to the back of the book, and you will find all of the templates that you need to make the projects. Enlarge the templates based on the percentages listed and then follow the individual project instructions for using them. If you have a scanner and printer, then you won't even need a trip to the copy shop!

cutting

The majority of these projects utilize a rotary cutter, a self-healing mat, and a clear quilting ruler or two. With these tools, you can easily create nice, neat shapes—squares, diamonds, and strips—for painless patchwork piecing. Of course, if freestyle is more your thing, a rotary cutter can help you zip through those fabrics like nobody's business!

When it comes to fussy cutting (focusing on a certain lovely bit of your fabric and cutting it out in a particular shape), your rotary cutter may not be nimble enough. In this case, you'll want to reach for a pair of super-sharp scissors to help liberate that one perfect piece of fabric (A).

sewing + piecing + patchwork

Yay! Now let's cozy up to that sewing machine, shall we? Whether this is your first attempt at making a quilt or you've already wrapped everyone in your family in a quilt-y embrace, the basic process is really as simple as 1, 2, and 3.

1 Take two pieces of fabric and pin one on top of the other with right sides facing.

2 Sew them together (B); generally a ¼-inch (6 mm) seam allowance is used. Seam allowance is the space between your stitched line and the raw edge of the fabric (C).

3 Press the seams open or to one side (usually to the side of the darker fabric) (D). You may be tempted to skip this step sometimes, but don't.

That's really it, from the simplest of patched squares to the most elaborately-pieced lovelies. Oh, and don't fret: for those intricately constructed quilties (you know which ones I'm talking about… they've already made you gasp!), the project instructions include information for cutting and piecing order.

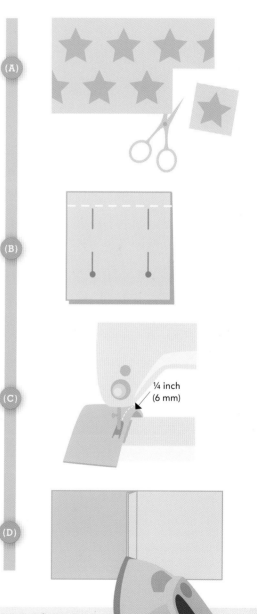

(A)

(B)

(C)

¼ inch (6 mm)

(D)

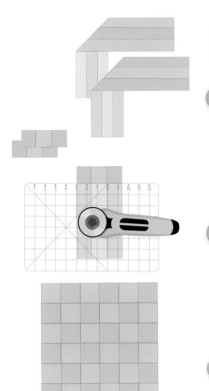

strips

Whether you're randomly stitching together fabric strips or perfectly piecing them, patchwork piecing is just so much fun, especially with strips! Use this quick tip for piecing strips that will have even a beginner looking like a patchwork pro.

1 Stitch a group of strips together. Press (E).

2 Cut those pieced strips into strips (F).

3 Now rotate the orientation of the pieces, stitch those very same strips together again (of course, you won't forget to press!), and prepare to be amazed at your patchwork speed and prowess (G). Way quicker than piecing a bunch of teeny 1-inch (2.5 cm) squares together!

And here's one technique that you'll want to keep in your patchwork bag-o'-tricks: chain piecing. Here's what to do: Simply feed your pieces through the sewing machine one after another, leaving a little space between them. When you're done, you'll have a lovely little "chain" of pieced bits that you can cut apart before continuing on to your next step.

english paper piecing

In the realm of English paper piecing, perfection and precision are fundamental. How can you have a nice, crisp hexagon without sharp angles and perfect corners? Well, simply put, you cannot. With the aid of paper templates and a few tips, you too can achieve shiny, happy hexagons, plus loads of other fun shapes!

1 First, carefully cut a number of paper templates, or you can save some time and find precut shapes online.

2 Place the templates on the wrong side of the fabric and cut around each, leaving a ¼-inch (6 mm) allowance on all sides (H).

3 Fold the seam allowance over the edges of the template (I), and then press them in place using a steam iron or just your fingers; I usually opt for the latter as it makes the project portable!

4 Baste the edges in place (J), working only through the fabric corners and edges or directly through the paper. I usually prefer the latter, which makes for lots of pin-pricked templates!

5 Give everything a good pressing when you're done for a crisp edge.

6 Once you've basted all of your hexagons, attach them, right sides together, at the edges (K) using a ladder stitch (page 13). Remove the paper templates.

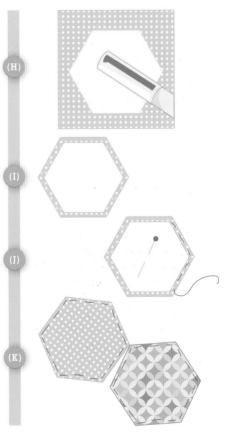

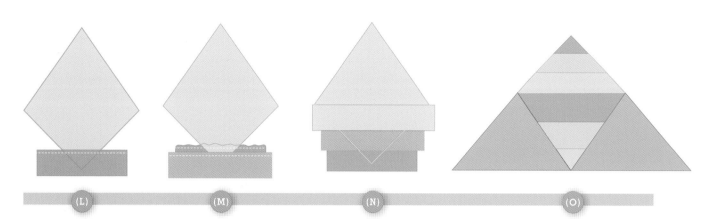

foundation piecing

Foundation piecing can be either temporary (using a paper template) or permanent (using a muslin or other fabric base). It's also a wonderful way to use up some of the tinier bits of your favorite fabrics. For this technique, the main idea is that you're sewing your pieces to a base layer, turning under the edges as you go.

1 Choose either a temporary paper or permanent fabric base and cut to the indicated size.

2 With your fabric strips close at hand, place the first strip of fabric right side up over the tip of the base. Stitch (L).

3 Place the second strip, wrong side up, on top of the first stitched strip, allowing an $1/8$ inch (.3 cm) of the top of the first strip to show. Stitch (M). Press up so that the right side is facing you.

4 Place the third strip on top of the second one, wrong side up. Stitch (N). Press up. Continue in this manner until the template is covered, pressing as you go.

5 Now, turn the patchwork-covered template over. Using a ruler and rotary cutter, trim the fabric edges flush with the template edges.

> **Tip** *If you're using a paper base, spritz the paper template with water and carefully tear the template along the stitch lines. Remove any stray paper bits and press your patchworked piece.*

6 Stitch the finished piece to its neighbors (O).

free-form + improvisational piecing

Ah, free-form and improvisational piecing. I must tell you that this may very well be my favorite way to work. I put my quilting ruler aside for a bit, grab a stack of scraps, pick up my rotary cutter, and just go for it. You will be surprised at how well you can freehand those cuts! And the knowledge that you don't have to be perfect is quite liberating—one of the reasons I so adore this technique. Grab, sew, cut, repeat...and repeat, and repeat. You may love it so much that you don't stop until you have actually made your quilt top! Of course, you get to square everything up as often as you want to (see page 14), depending on how you feel about "wonky" (love the term or hate it, it seems to be part of a modern sewist's vocabulary). Personally, I am more about the understated, unintentional wonk...or a little bit of purposeful wonky that appears to be totally natural (at least, that's what I tell myself when I'm sewing and I don't feel like being persnickety about measuring). To wonk or not to wonk, or to what degree you want to take the wonkiness, is totally up to you. Want to see some free-form piecing in action? See A+ doll quilt (page 68), Arches (page 32), or Scrappy Asterisks (page 112).

appliqué

When it comes to the bang-for-your-buck on the embellishment scene, appliqué is where it's at! And it's so much fun to mix it with patchwork. Truly, the possibilities are almost endless, especially if you have an eye for freehand. If not, you can be confident that the project templates will make you look like you do. When it comes to adhering your appliqué shape to the base fabric, a temporary fabric spray adhesive or iron-on fusible web will hold your shape in place while you stitch. Hmmm, now which stitch to use?

(P)   (Q)   (R)

A **simple straight stitch** can do the job easily while leaving the edges raw, or try a tight **zigzag stitch** for a bolder line that also protects the appliqué edges from fraying in the wash (P).

Sketch stitching is a fun way to adhere your appliqué shape, too. Begin by outlining the shape about ¼ inch (6 mm) in from the edge. Continue to go over this line a few times (no need for perfection here!), a little more to the outer edge and then a little more to the inside, crossing back and forth over your original line for a "sketched" look (Q).

For a crisp, neat edge, you may want to try the **needle turn method**. This one is a favorite technique of mine since it makes a project portable. Here's how: First, trace your appliqué template onto the back of your fabric. Cut out the shape, adding a ⅛-inch (3 mm) allowance around each edge. Pinch and press the fabric along the traced line, and baste the shape to the base fabric. Then attach the edges with a blind stitch (opposite page). It may take a bit of practice, but when you've got the hang of it, the stitches will virtually be invisible. Truth be told, I'm one of those people who actually finds this relaxing (along with hand-stitching quilt bindings, which we will get to in a moment) (R).

embroidery

Is there any more perfect form of portable sewing? I think not! There is just something so right about the sound of needle poking fabric and thread swishing its way through. Don't you know that there's an extra little bit of magic that occurs when embroidery and quilting are combined? A hand-embroidered initial on a keepsake quilt pieced from bits of a dear one's gown, a wee redcap just begging to be plucked from Baba Yaga's forest, or a favorite fairy tale darling in a smartly stitched cloak...it is amazing what effect simple stitches and colorful floss can have! Be sure to refer to each project for the number of strands (ply) to use.

transferring patterns + prepping fabric

The simplest (and my preferred) method to transfer an embroidery pattern to fabric involves three things: a sunny window, tape, and a water soluble pen. Tape the pattern to the window. Tape the fabric over it. Trace. Easy! Of course, a lightbox is also an excellent choice (if you happen to have one lying about), especially if your fabric is darker in color. Fabric transfer paper, pens, and pencils are also an option. Now is the time to hoop up your fabric (plastic, wood, you decide!) as we review some common stitches.

stitches

What is a sweet little quilt without some hand-stitched loveliness? And yes, even the utilitarian stitches are lovely when done by a caring hand! This handy dandy stitch chart is here to inspire (and maybe refresh your memory, too).

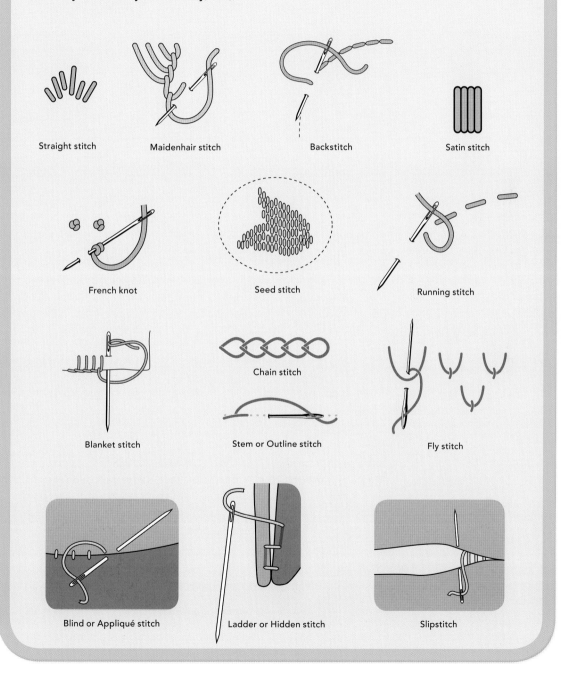

Straight stitch

Maidenhair stitch

Backstitch

Satin stitch

French knot

Seed stitch

Running stitch

Blanket stitch

Chain stitch

Stem or Outline stitch

Fly stitch

Blind or Appliqué stitch

Ladder or Hidden stitch

Slipstitch

quilting

Use your tried-and-true method or sample a new-to-you technique; doll quilts are perfect opportunities to perfect or stretch your quilting repertoire.

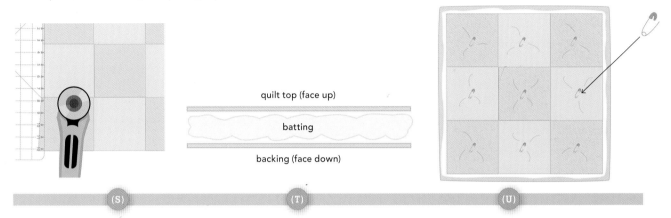

quilt top (face up)

batting

backing (face down)

(S) (T) (U)

the quilt sandwich!

Well, we are finally here. One yummy quilt sandwich coming right up! First things first, be sure that your quilt top and backing are freshly pressed. Next, square up (S) any edges or corners of your quilt. On a flat surface, lay the quilt backing wrong side up. You may want to secure the edges with a bit of quilter's tape, though painter's tape works fine, too! Place the batting on top, smoothing it out from the center. Next comes the quilt top, right side up in all of its glory (T). Secure all three layers with basting pins (if using basting spray, please follow the manufacturer's instructions), beginning in the center and working outward to the edges, smoothing as you go (U).

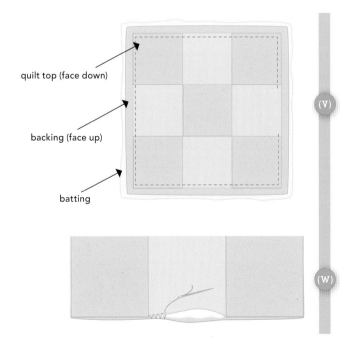

quilt top (face down)

backing (face up)

batting

(V)

(W)

If you're planning on using the **quick-turn method**, here's a quick look at how to alternately stack your quilt sandwich (hold the binding, please!).

1 Lay the batting down first, then the quilt backing (right side up), followed by the quilt top (right side down). Smooth each layer as you go (V).

2 Pin around the outside edge, smoothing as you go.

3 Using a ½-inch (1.3 cm) seam allowance, stitch around the outside edge of the quilt, leaving an 6-inch (15.2 cm) opening for turning.

4 With a rotary cutter or scissors, carefully trim the layers along the edges and across the corners to decrease the bulk.

5 Turn the quilt right side out. Handstitch the opening closed (W).

6 Quilt as desired.

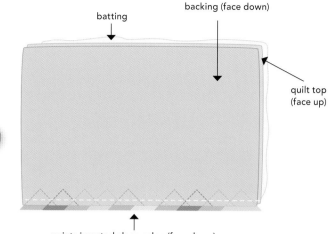

batting

backing (face down)

quilt top (face up)

(X)

points inserted along edge (face down)

If you're planning to insert **prairie points**, you'll use pretty much the same method with a slight alteration. First, stack your layers as follows: batting, quilt top (right side up), prairie points (right side down), and backing (right side down) (X). Stitch around the edges, leaving an opening for turning, and assemble as you would for the quick-turn method.

stitching

Now here is where your quilty truly comes into being…in the quilting! Will you be hand-stitching? Tying? Using your sewing machine? A combination of the three? Whatever method you choose, it will bring a certain feeling and mood to your finished quilt. If you have a walking foot for your machine, now would be the time to put it on and cue the celestial chorus. Seriously, for straight line quilting (and sewing on binding), this attachment will change your life!

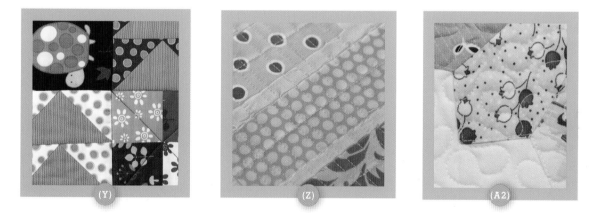

(Y)

(Z)

(A2)

Stitch in the Ditch: If you want your quilting to be virtually invisible, allowing the fabrics to take center-stage, you may want to "stitch in the ditch" by actually stitching into the seams of the patchworked fabric (Y).

Straight Line Stitching: Stitch vertical and/or horizontal straight lines, preferably with a walking foot. I'm not kidding—it is that good. But, ahem, the lines don't have to be perfectly straight, really. You can use a quilting bar attachment for perfectly spaced quilting lines. Alternately, your quilting ruler and water soluble pen are perfect for drawing guidelines (Z).

Free-Motion Stitching: Drop your feed dogs, add a darning foot, and go to town! Guide the quilt sandwich through the sewing machine to create an all-over stippling pattern (A2), or try your hand at pebble quilting (see the sidebar on page 16). Anything goes.

(B2) (C2)

Hand Quilting: As beautiful as machine quilting can be, there is just nothing like the look of hand-quilting. I won't kid you; it takes some time. But one of the wonderful aspects of making a doll-sized quilt is just that: It's small. It won't take a year to complete. It's doable. If you want to practice hand-quilting, well, here you go (B2).

Tying: Simple, tactile, a nod to days gone by...and perfect if a kiddo is making this quilt with you for a treasured doll or softie. Choose from embroidery floss, wool yarn, or perle cotton. Down in one spot, up almost right beside it, and then tie the tails in a square knot. Trim the ends suitably (C2).

pebble quilting

Brioni Greenberg offers these words of wisdom: Pebble quilting is a very simple technique that looks much more complicated than it actually is.

1 Start the design at any area of the quilt you wish. First stitch a figure "8."

2 Continue to fill the space between the two circles with further circles. You may find that practicing drawing it out on a piece of paper helps you.

3 Continue and continue some more!

This is intended to be a continuous pattern so there will be times when you need to go back over a circle that you have already created to complete the circle or get to the next area you wish. The extra stitching will just enhance the circles. As you work, alter the size of the pebbles to fill the space you have and avoid quilting an area unintentionally.

the finishing touches

You've cut, pieced, stitched, pressed, quilted, and BAM...made a quilt top! Think of this part of the process as sticking those frilly, colorful little toothpicks into your "sandwich."

binding

Ah, binding! Strong opinions exist when it comes to binding. Some dread this step (in which case, see the sidebar on page 19), and others relish it. Either way, we can all smile happily together as we know that we are only a few short steps from finishing up.

make your own
Making your own binding is really quite simple.

1 To figure out how long of a piece you will need for a particular quilt, add together the lengths of the edges you are binding, plus about 4 to 6 inches (10.2 to 15.2 cm) extra.

2 Refer to the project instructions for the recommended width of the binding strip: 2 to 3 inches (5 to 7.6 cm) are common widths. Cut strips (preferably on the bias) from fabric or stitch several strips together to make a binding strip long enough for your project. Pin and stitch the short ends of your strips together, right sides facing. Press the seams open.

If you're using one fabric to make your binding strip, join and stitch the ends at a 45° angle (D2). For patchworked binding, the ends are generally joined end to end (E2).

3 With wrong sides together, fold your binding strip in half, lengthwise. Press.

double-fold (or french) binding
In my estimation, double-fold binding is simply the way to go. Not only are you giving your little doll quilt another layer of protection against wear and tear, but it's just so darn pleasant to work with! Don't let the process intimidate you. In fact, after you have successfully bound a few doll quilts, you may even secretly (or not so secretly!) start to love this final step. I know I do!

1 Pin your newly-made binding strip (already folded and pressed in half lengthwise, wrong sides together) to the right side of the quilt top, lining up the raw edges.

2 Starting about 5 inches (12.7 cm) from the end of the binding strip (F2), stitch in place using the recommended seam allowance—typically ¼ inch (.6 cm)—stopping ¼ inch (.6 cm) from the first corner. Backstitch a few times to secure the thread. Clip the thread and remove the quilt from the sewing machine.

3 To miter the corner, fold the binding strip up at 45° toward the top of the quilt. Fold the strip back down and align it with the next side of the quilt. Begin stitching again (G2), ¼ inch (.6 cm) in from the folded edge.

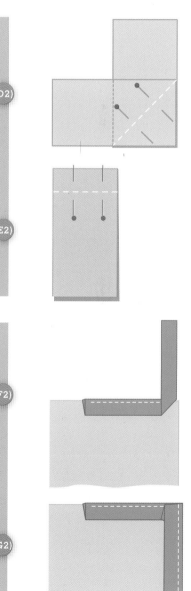

(D2)

(E2)

(F2)

(G2)

4 Continue stitching the binding along the quilt's edge, mitering each corner as you get to it.

5 Stop stitching about 6 inches (15.2 cm) from your starting point. Backstitch. Clip the threads and remove the quilt from the machine. Overlap the ends of the binding strips and stitch them with right sides together. Cut the excess and press the seam open.

6 Stitch down this last section of the binding.

7 Fold the binding to the back of the quilt. Hold it in place (you can always pin it, if you'd like) and slipstitch the binding to the backside of the quilt, mitering the corners as you get to them.

Still not convinced that you'll love hand-stitching the binding onto your quilt? Well, put down the needle and thread and head back on over to the sewing machine. Once you've attached the double-fold binding to the front of the quilt, dampen it slightly with a spray bottle and fold it around to the back of the quilt, pinning carefully. With invisible thread in the bobbin and matching cotton thread up top, topstitch the binding to the back of the quilt. You'll end up with a nearly invisible stitch line in the ditch on the front of the quilt!

butted corners

If you're short on time, butted corners may suit your quilt just fine. In fact, this method of binding is actually quick and easy when done completely on the sewing machine! It's also a good choice if you're short on fabric: Instead of one long binding strip, you can use separate pieces for each edge.

1 Working one edge at a time, pin and then stitch binding along the two short edges on the right side of the quilt (H2).

2 Fold the binding to the back (if it's single-fold, tuck under the raw edge), and then stitch it down on the back of the quilt using a slipstitch or stitching in the ditch of the seam you just created.

3 Measure and cut the length that you'll need for the other two edges of the quilt. Be sure to add a little extra to each end. Attach the binding to the edges as you did previously.

4 Turn under the extra binding at each end and use a slipstitch to close the ends (I2). Alternately, do this on your sewing machine, making sure to backstitch at the beginning and end.

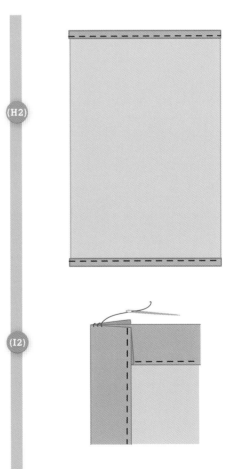

labels

A sweet little label attached to the backside of your quilt not only lets you take credit for the loveliness that you've created but can also add a happy surprise. I'm usually not organized enough (yes, I'm admitting it!) to piece the label into the back of the quilt—and really, I like to save the label for the very last bit. Often I will hand-stitch an element from the quilt or a little something meant especially for the recipient. Of course, rubber stamps and permanent ink, permanent marking pens, and printable fabric are all options for creating labels, too (J2).

washing and hanging

I absolutely adore the crinkly quality of a freshly washed and dried quilt, no matter the size! However, if crisp and pristine makes you giddy, then by all means skip the washing and drying. When it comes to hanging our doll quilts on the wall, keep it simple: Straight pins (I apologize if some of you are cringing now!) or painter's tape does the trick for me. In our home, a little quilty is just as likely to decorate the wall as it is to swaddle a softie…ah, the awesomeness of the doll quilt!

(J2)

how you, too, can love binding: three heartfelt suggestions

If you're not a fan of this portion of our program, please, indulge me in a little public service announcement about binding and how you can love it more!

- Choose a luscious fabric that you adore and that compliments your work. It will look smashing, and you can gaze at it lovingly as you stitch it to your quilt.

- Choose many luscious fabrics and make a patchy strip for binding! You won't be able to take your eyes off of its loveliness as you stitch.

- Find a comfy spot (preferably under a larger quilt), listen to your favorite music (or the sounds of silence once the house has gone to sleep!), and lose yourself in the repetitive, meditative magic that is hand-stitching the binding onto the back of a quilt.

mod log cabin

Impromptu piecing and embroidery work together perfectly in this cute little quilt.

handmade by **CATHY GAUBERT**

fabric & such

1 piece of linen for center embroidery, 10 inches square (25.4 cm)

Red embroidery floss

½ yard (.5 m) total of assorted red, white, and gray fabrics

½ yard (.5 m) of backing fabric

1 piece of batting, 24 inches square (61 cm)

tools

Basic Patchwork Kit (page 8)

Templates (page 123)

Fray retardant (optional)

finished size

21½ x 23 inches (54.6 x 58.4 cm)

seam allowance

¼ inch (6 mm)

get started

1 Enlarge the embroidery template and trace it onto the 10-inch (25.4 cm) center square. Using a simple backstitch and two strands of floss, embroider the girls and embellish with French knots.

2 Gently wash the marker out of your embroidered piece, per the manufacturer's directions, and allow it to dry. Trim the square to 7 x 8½ inches (17.8 x 21.6 cm).

3 While your embroidered piece is drying, use the rotary cutter and ruler to cut the assorted fabrics into strips that measure 3 inches (7.6 cm) wide x the length of the fabric. You will need a total of 12 strips for the quilt top. How many strips of each fabric will depend on how many fabrics you are using. It's a good idea to cut a bunch; you'll have more choices when you begin piecing your log cabin. If you like, lay out the strips around the embroidery (**A**).

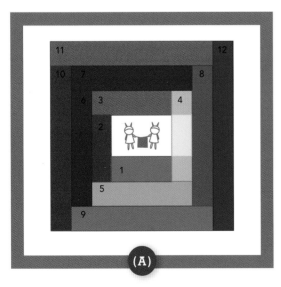

(A)

4 Now start building the cabin.

- With your trimmed embroidery piece face up, place strip 1 face down, matching up the bottom edges. Stitch and press open. Trim if necessary (this is where you can wonkify your block a bit by slightly turning your pieced top before you square it up).

- Continue adding strips to the block in a clockwise manner (following the diagram) until you have used all 12 strips. (Of course, you can add more or fewer strips, to make a larger or smaller doll quilt). Be sure to trim and press as you go.

> *If you like, you can scrap-piece some of the strips for effect or out of necessity.*

5 Square up the quilt top, if needed. Make a quilt sandwich of the backing, batting, and quilt top, then pin or baste all layers in place. Quilt by machine or by hand in horizontal or vertical lines. Add other hand stitching as you like, for example the vertical lines of running stitches around the girls.

6 To make the teeny quilt, cut one piece of gray approximately 1½ x 2 inches (3.8 x 5 cm) and one piece of red just a smidge smaller. Use fray retardant on the edges and let dry. Stitch the red piece to the gray one. Cut a tiny square for the cabin and a tiny triangle for the roof from gray scraps. Stitch them into place on the red square. Tack the teeny cabin quilt right below each girls' hand.

If you plan on washing your doll quilt, you may want to attach the teeny quilt afterwards.

7 Cut strips using your red and gray fabrics; trim your leftover scraps to 2½ inches (6.4 cm) wide by varying lengths. Sew the red scraps end to end to make a patchwork binding strip, measuring against the red side of the quilt to get an approximate length. Do the same with the gray pieces, and then join the two strips together. Measure the binding strip against the quilt again (being sure to miter the corners just as you do when you sew the binding on) and then attach the binding (page 17). If you measured well, the binding and the quilt should match up nicely.

cupcake quilt

Like cupcakes, the hexagons in this quilt are a perfect little treat. Simple piecing tips will help you whip them up in no time.

handmade by **MALKA DUBRAWSKY**

fabric & such

Scraps of assorted fabric, at least 3 x 7 inches (7.6 x 17.8 cm)

¾ yard (.7 m) of cream fabric

1 yard (.9 m) of coordinating fabric for backing

1 yard (.9 m) of batting

tools

Basic Patchwork Kit (page 8)

Templates (page 121)

Office paper for templates

finished size

27 x 23¾ inches (68.6 x 60.3 cm)

seam allowance

¼ inch (6 mm) unless otherwise noted.

note: *Press all the seams to one side, alternating sides where the seams intersect.*

get started

1 From scraps of fabric:

- Cut 12 strips measuring 1 x 7 inches (2.5 x 17.8 cm).

- Cut 24 strips measuring 3 x 7 inches (7.6 x 17.8 cm).

2 Enlarge and cut out all the templates. From cream fabric:

- Cut 12 strips measuring 3 x 7 inches (7.6 x 17.8 cm).

- Cut 24 strips measuring 1¼ x 7 inches (3.2 x 17.8 cm).

- Using template B, cut 24 diamonds.

- Using template C, cut 16 triangles.

- Cut binding strips measuring 1½ inches (3.8 cm) wide.

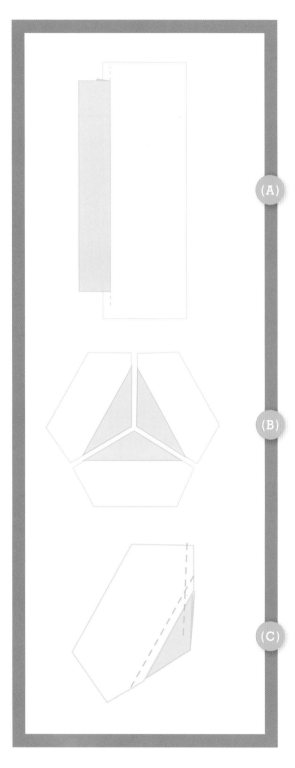

(A)

(B)

(C)

3 To make the light-colored hexagons for the centers:

- Pin a 1 x 7-inch (2.5 x 17.8 cm) scrap fabric strip to a 3 x 7-inch (7.6 x 17.8 cm) cream fabric strip, right sides together along long edges as shown (**A**). Stitch together and press the seam.

- Working on a cutting mat, place template A on a stitched pair, right side facing up, with the point of the template meeting the raw edge of the scrap fabric. Using a rotary cutter, cut around template A.

- Repeat to make a total of three template A pieces (**B**).

- Pin piece 1 to piece 2, right sides together, along the common edge. Starting at the outer corner, stitch the pieces together, stopping ¼ inch (6 mm) short of the corner. Backstitch to secure the seam. Press the seam.

- Stitch pieces 2 and 3 together in the same way (**C**).

- Realign and pin piece 3 to piece 1 and stitch together as before.

- Make a total of 4 center hexagons. Set aside.

4 To make the outer hexagons, pin the 3 x 7-inch (7.6 x 17.8 cm) scrap fabric strips to the 1¼ x 7-inch (3.2 x 17.8 cm) cream fabric strips with right sides together along the long edges. Stitch together and press the seam. Use template A to cut three pieces and stitch them together as with the center hexagons in step 3. Make a total of 24 outer hexagon pieces. Set aside.

5 To construct each block (for a total of 4 blocks), collect one center hexagon, six outer hexagons, six cream fabric diamonds, and four cream fabric triangles.

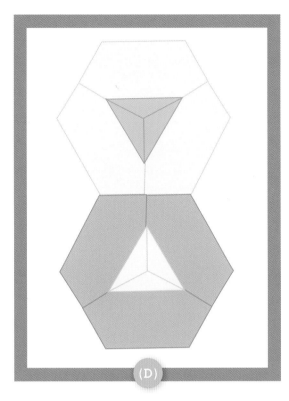

(D)

- Working with the center hexagon and one outer hexagon, pin pieces right sides together along a common edge. Starting ¼ inch (6 mm) from one edge, stitch the hexagons together, stopping ¼ inch (6 mm) from the opposite edge. Press the seam (D).

- Pin the second outer hexagon to the stitched pair, right sides together, along one common edge. Starting ¼ inch (6 mm) from an outside edge, stitch the hexagons together, stopping ¼ inch (6 mm) from the corner. Cut the thread. Realign and pin the second common edge to the stitched pair and stitch in the same way. Press the seams.

- Continue pinning, stitching, and pressing outer hexagons to complete a ring of six hexagons.

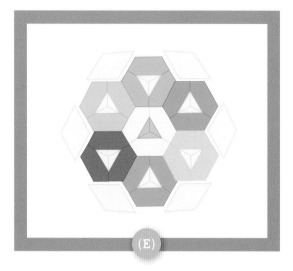

(E)

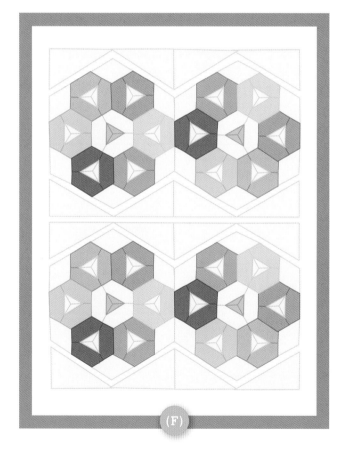

(F)

- Pin one cream fabric diamond to the sewn hexagons, right sides together, along one common edge, making sure that ¼ inch (6 mm) of the diamond extends beyond the hexagon edge (E). Starting at an outer corner, stitch toward the inner corner, stopping ¼ inch (6 mm) short. Cut the thread. Realign and pin the remaining edge of the diamond to the adjoining hexagon and stitch in the same way. Press the seam.

- Attach the remaining diamonds in the same way.

- Pin one cream fabric triangle to the sewn hexagon sections, right sides together along a long edge of the triangle, making sure points of the triangle extend a generous ¼ inch (6 mm) beyond the hexagon blocks. Stitch together and press the seams. Attach the remaining triangles in the same way (F).

> **Tip** *The triangles are intended to square off each hexagon block and are attached to four opposite corners of a block.*

6 To sew the blocks together, pin two blocks, right sides together, along a common edge. Stitch together and press the seam. Stitch together a second pair of blocks in the same way and press. Pin the sewn block pairs right sides together along long edges and stitch together. Press the seam.

7 Make a quilt sandwich of the backing, batting, and quilt top, then pin or baste all layers in place. Quilt by machine or by hand. The sample shows free-motion machine quilting in concentric ovals spaced about ¼ inch (6 mm) apart.

8 Square up the edges. Using scraps and diagonal seams, stitch together binding strips and attach the binding to quilt (see page 17).

A is for apples

Gather up a little basketful of red and green scraps to paper piece everyone's favorite fruit.

handmade by AMANDA WOODWARD-JENNINGS

fabric & such

½ yard (.5 m) of fabric for background

Red, cream, and green fabric scraps, each at least 5 inches (12.7 cm) tall

1 strip of wood grain fabric, 2½ x 17 inches (6.4 x 43.2 cm)

Scraps of green wool felt for the leaves and seeds

1 fat quarter (45.7 x 55.9 cm) of fabric for backing

1 piece of batting, 16 x 18 inches (40.6 x 45.7 cm)

¼ yard (.23 m) of fabric for binding

tools

Basic Patchwork Kit (page 8)

Templates (page 120)

Paper for paper piecing

Fabric adhesive

Spray starch

Seam ripper (optional)

finished size

15 x 17½ inches (38.1 x 44.5 cm)

seam allowance

¼ inch (6 mm)

get started

1 Enlarge and cut out the piecing templates, leaving an extra margin of paper outside the ¼-inch (6 mm) seam allowance to allow for squaring up the pieced sections later.

2 Adjust the stitch length on your sewing machine to about 1 or 1.5 mm. The shorter the stitch length, the easier it will be to remove the paper piecing templates.

3 Starting with the stems, select a brown fabric scrap and a scrap of the background fabric, and foundation paper piece (page 11) three stem sections, one for each apple. (The leaves will be added later as appliqué patches.)

> **Tip** You might want to stick your fabric pieces to the paper with fabric adhesive for this step; the stem can be finicky!

4 Following the piecing order on the apple template, start at one edge and stitch scraps across the apple in various shades of reds. You can make it as scrappy or as solid as you'd like. When the stitched piece is wide enough, add the corner angles from background fabric. Sew the remaining apple and half-apple in the same way, using the templates as a guide.

5 Square up the finished apples and stems. With the printed/sewn lines facing up, use a rotary cutter and clear ruler to trim along the dotted lines.

6 With the paper still attached to the apples, give each patchwork piece a spray of starch and press well. Then carefully remove the paper, making sure not to pull up any of your stitches. As long as you used a shortened stitch length as instructed in step 2, you should have no problems. You can also run the edge of a seam ripper along the edge of the stitching to make it easier to remove the paper.

7 To attach the stems to the apples, change the sewing machine back to a standard stitch length, approximately 2.5 mm. With right sides together, pin a stem piece to the top of an apple and stitch. Press the seam open or to one side. This apple is now complete. Stitch the remaining apples in the same way, following the template lines.

8 Decide the order you like best for your apples. Cut two 2½ x 5-inch (6.4 x 12.7 cm) strips and stitch them on both sides of the middle apple, and then stitch the other apples on to either side of those strips. Cut two additional 2½ x 5-inch (6.4 x 12.7 cm) strips of fabric and sew one at the beginning and one at the end of the apple strip. Press the seams.

9 Create a table for the apples by stitching the strip of wood grain fabric to the bottom of the apple row, right sides facing, using a ¼-inch (6 mm) seam allowance. Press the seam.

10 For the bottom of the quilt, cut a 2½ x 17-inch (6.4 x 43.2 cm) strip from the background fabric. With right sides facing, stitch it to the bottom of the wood grain strip, then press the seams as before.

11 Cut a piece of background fabric that measures 7 x 17 inches (17.8 x 43.2 cm). Sew it to the top of the apple strip in the same way as the bottom strip in step 10.

12 To create the leaves, cut four leaflike shapes from the green wool felt and machine stitch them next to each apple. Attach the seeds in the same way. To keep the pieces in place when sewing, spray the back of the felt with fabric adhesive, press it onto the fabric, then stitch the leaf in place.

13 Make a quilt sandwich of the backing, batting, and quilt top, then pin or baste all layers in place. Quilt as desired.

14 Cut strips from the binding fabric and bind the quilt (page 17).

arches

You'll never be intimidated by curves again with this neat technique for piecing scrappy curved strips.

handmade by JESSICA BERRETT

fabric & such

1 piece of lightweight linen or linen/cotton blend fabric (starched and pressed), 21 x 27 inches (53.3 x 68.6 cm)

1 piece of multicolored theme fabric, 12 x 13 inches (30.5 x 33 cm)

Scraps of assorted fabrics in coordinating colors, 2 to 4-inch squares and rectangles (5.1 to 10.2 cm)

1 piece of whole or scrap-pieced backing fabric, 21 x 20 inches (53.3 x 50.8 cm)

1 piece of batting, 21 x 27 inches (53.3 x 68.6 cm)

¼ yard (.23 m) of coordinating binding fabric

tools

Basic Patchwork Kit (page 8)

finished size

23 x 17½ inches (58.4 x 44.5 cm)

seam allowance

¼ inch (6 mm)

get started

1 Lay the starched linen piece, right side up, on the rotary cutting mat. Place the theme fabric rectangle over the linen, right side up, in the upper right corner. Use the rotary cutter and a small ruler to cut a smooth curve through both layers, gently sliding the ruler along as you cut the curve (**A**).

2 Discard the piece of linen under the theme fabric, as well as the cut-off corner of theme fabric. Use a disappearing fabric marker to make a few matching marks along the curve, on each fabric edge.

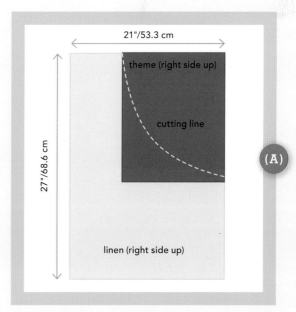

21"/53.3 cm

theme (right side up)

cutting line

27"/68.6 cm

linen (right side up)

(A)

3 Pin the curves you just cut, right sides together, matching the marks you made (B). Stitch the curve slowly, with ¼-inch (6 mm) seam allowance. Clip the seam allowance as needed and press the seam open.

4 Cut 15 to 20 small coordinating scrap pieces into slight trapezoid shapes (straight sides, angled in at the bottom). Some square sides are okay, too. They should all be about the same width, but different lengths.

5 Lay the quilt top, right side up, on your cutting mat. Arrange the scraps, right side up, into a pleasing arch shape. Due to seam allowances, you will need to make it longer than the quilt top. Stitch the scraps, right sides together, into an arched strip. Lay the arch over the quilt top from time to time, to check your progress and length. Do not worry about uneven edges.

6 Arrange the arch, right side up, on top of the quilt top. Use the rotary cutter and a ruler to cut a smooth curve along the top edge of the arch (C). Discard the scrap trimmings, but keep the detached piece of linen (set it aside for now).

(B)

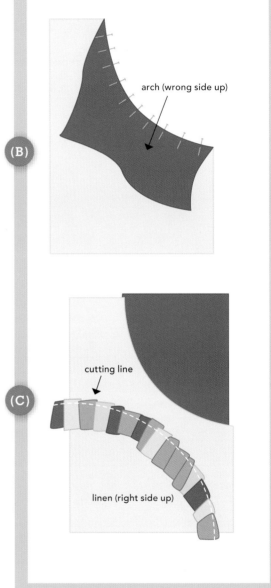

arch (wrong side up)

(C)

cutting line

linen (right side up)

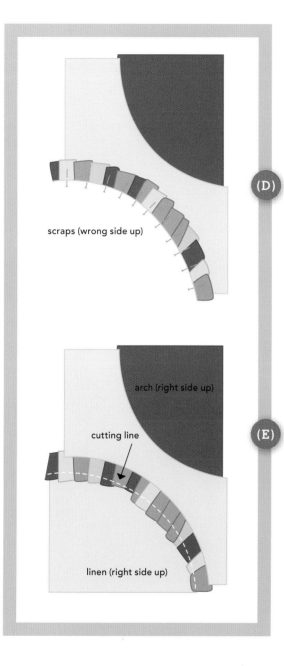

scraps (wrong side up)

(D)

arch (right side up)

cutting line

linen (right side up)

(E)

7 As before, use a fabric marker to make a few matching marks along the curve on each fabric edge. Pin the curves, right sides together, matching the marks you made **(D)**. Stitch the curve slowly, then clip the seam allowance and press the seam open.

8 Lay the quilt top on the cutting mat. Slip the curved edge of the linen piece (set aside in step 6) just under the uneven lower edge of the scrap arch. Use your rotary cutter and ruler as before to cut a curve along the bottom edge of the scrap arch, through both layers **(E)**. Discard the scrap and linen trimmings from under the arch. Make marks, match up edges, and stitch as before, then press the seams.

9 Repeat steps 5 through 8 to create a second smaller arch in the lower left corner, below the first.

10 Square up the edges (page 14) and trim the quilt top into an 24 x 18-inch (61 x 45.7 cm) rectangle. Make a quilt sandwich of the backing, batting, and quilt top, and then pin or baste all layers in place. Quilt by machine or by hand as desired; or you could tie it for a different look.

11 Cut 2-inch-wide (5.1 cm) strips from the binding fabric and bind the quilt (page 17).

chevron arrows

This clever quilt will have you loving prairie points, and it's much easier to construct than it first appears thanks to appliquéd shapes.

handmade by SUSAN SOBON

fabric & such

1 fat quarter (45.7 x 55.9 cm) of dark, printed fabric for background

5 pieces of bright printed fabric, each ⅛ yard (.23 m)

1 piece of double-sided fusible web, at least 8 x 20 inches (20.3 x 50.8 cm)

1 fat quarter (45.7 x 55.9 cm) of fabric for backing (in sample, the background and backing fabrics are the same)

1 piece of batting or plain flannel, 14 x 24 inches (35.6 x 61 cm)

tools

Basic Patchwork Kit (page 8)

Spray starch (optional)

finished size

11 x 20¾ inches (27.9 x 52.7 cm)

seam allowance

¼ inch (6 mm)

get started

1 Cut the background fabric into an 11 x 20½-inch (27.9 x 52.1 cm) rectangle. Set aside.

2 Cut the bright fabrics into strips that are 1¼ inches (3.2 cm) wide x half the width of the fabric. Decide the order of the fabrics and label the corner of each strip accordingly: A for the tip of each arrow, then B, C, D, and E for the widest end.

3 Lay out the strips on the fusible web, side by side with no space in between. Take care to keep the strips straight and trim off any ends that are longer than the web. Fuse the strips all at once to the web, then use a rotary cutter and quilting ruler to separate the strips.

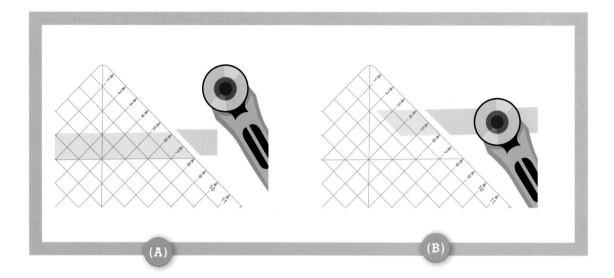

(A) (B)

4 To cut a diamond, lay your ruler on one strip with the 45° angle line along the bottom of your strip. Slice the end off the strip (A). Flip the strip with the "tail" going toward the right. Line up the angled edge on the 1¼-inch (3.2 cm) mark and cut (B). Cut out diamonds as follows:

- From A fabric: 3
- From B fabric: 6
- From C fabric: 9
- From D fabric: 12
- From E fabric: 15

5 Peel off the paper backing from the diamonds, keeping track of the A–E colors.

6 Fold the background fabric in half crosswise to locate the center line and lightly press. Center the first A diamond with its top point on the center line 1¼ inches (3.2 cm) from the top edge. Fuse in place according to the manufacturer's directions. Add the remaining diamonds in order, leaving a small gap between each diamond, pressing them down as you go.

7 With the central diamond in place, fold each short end of the background fabric to the center line and press lightly. These will be the new center lines for the diamonds on either side. Turn the quilt top so the "arrow" is now pointing toward you. Build the new arrows in the same way as the first one; you might want to lay out all of the diamonds before fusing, to make sure the rows are aligned and fit well on the background. Leave about an inch (2.5 cm) between your arrow shapes.

8 When all the diamonds are fused, edgestitch around each one with a straight, buttonhole, or satin stitch.

9 To make the prairie points for the edging, cut 2½-inch (6.4 cm) squares from each of the bright fabrics. You will need a total of 36 squares. Fold each square in half on the diagonal to make a triangle, then press. Fold again on the diagonal to make a smaller triangle and press again. Use spray starch to stiffen the fabric, if you like.

10 To attach the prairie points:

- With the background fabric right side up, start on one long edge by pinning a prairie point with the raw edges matching and the opening toward the right. Alternating colors, pin the next prairie point, facing the same way as the first, with the new point under the first point. Overlapping in this way will make the stitching go more smoothly.

- At the end of the first edge, you will want the prairie point to end in the corner. Go back and adjust the overlapping points as needed so that the final points align with the corner, then stitch the row.

- To start the next row, abut the first prairie point against the last point on the previous edge (C). Overlap the points in this row as before, adjusting at the corners as needed, and stitch.

- Work your way around the background fabric until you've stitched prairie points to all four sides.

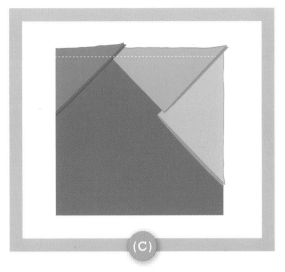

(C)

11 At this point, you could add the backing and batting, and finish the quilt. But here's an option for a more interesting back side to the quilt. Piece a strip of half-triangles as follows:

- Select four of the bright fabrics and cut two 2½-inch (6.4 cm) squares from each.

- From the fifth bright fabric, cut 3 strips that each measure 1¼ x 3½ inches (3.2 x 8.9 cm).

- From the backing fabric, cut 2 strips that each measure 1½ x 3½ inches (3.8 x 8.9 cm).

- Lay a square on top of a different-colored square, right sides facing, and draw a line diagonally down the center from corner to opposite corner. Stitch ¼ inch (6 mm) on

both sides of this line, then cut on the line (D). Press open. You now have two blocks composed of stitched triangles. Repeat this step with the remaining squares to complete eight stitched blocks.

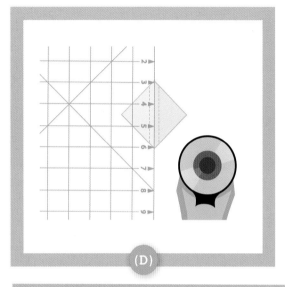

(D)

■ Match up the blocks in groups of 4 to make two new blocks. Join the rows together. Lay out the strips and blocks as shown (E), and stitch together.

12 From the backing fabric, cut one 7 x 13-inch (17.8 x 33 cm) piece and one 13-inch square (33 cm). Stitch these pieces to either side of the half-triangle strip to form a complete backing for the quilt. Press, and then trim to size as needed to match the quilt top.

13 To finish the quilt, follow the quick turn method (page 14) and make a quilt sandwich of the batting, quilt top (face up), and backing (face down). Stitch on all sides with a seam slightly wider than the prairie points stitch line, leaving a 5- to 6-inch (12.7 to 15.2 cm) gap for turning. Clip the corners and turn right side out, pushing out the corners. Press, and hand-sew the opening closed with a slipstitch.

14 Quilt as desired.

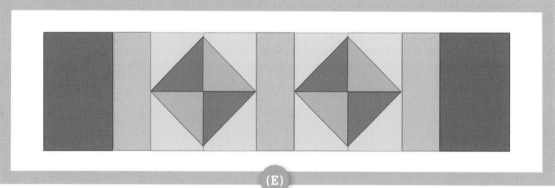

(E)

patchy beetle

A neat blend of patchwork and appliqué makes up the design for this perfect specimen.

handmade by **REBEKA LAMBERT**

fabric & such

Scraps of assorted fabric

¼ yard (.23 m or cm) of white fabric

½ yard (.5 m) of dark fabric for the background

⅛ yard (.15 m) of dotted print fabric

¾ yard (.7 m) of backing fabric

¾ yard (.7 m) of batting

tools

Basic Patchwork Kit (page 8)

Templates (page 120)

Paper for paper piecing

finished size

23½ x 19 inches (59.7 x 48.3 cm)

seam allowance

¼ inch (6 mm)

get started

1 Enlarge the paper templates for the beetle, and add ¼ inch (6 mm) seam allowance around the edges of each piece. Cut them out. Flip the body piece over and cut a second body piece that is a mirror image of the first.

2 Use the foundation paper piecing method (page 11) to apply an assortment of fabric scraps to the body pieces and the head piece. When the paper pieces are fully covered, trim the edges flush with the seam allowance. Tear away the paper. Set these pieces aside.

3 Use the templates to cut out six legs, two antennae, and the two remaining head pieces from single pieces of fabric.

4 Assemble the beetle pieces on white fabric and pin in place. Hand sew the beetle pieces to the white fabric by turning under the edges of the appliqué ¼ inch (6 mm) with the tip of your needle as you secure with a blind stitch. When the body and head pieces have been sewn on, trim around the beetle, leaving ½ inch (1.3 cm) of white fabric as a border on all sides.

5 Cut a 13 x 20-inch (33 x 50.8 cm) piece of the dark background fabric. Center the appliqué on this piece and hand sew with a blind stitch as in step 4.

6 Position the legs and antennae around the beetle, pin in place, and hand sew. Once the appliqué is complete, trim the background piece to 11 x 17½ inches (27.9 x 44.5 cm).

7 From the dotted fabric, cut two strips that are 2 inches (5.1 cm) x the width of the fabric. Stitch the strips to the top and bottom of the background fabric, then trim the strips even with the side edges. Stitch the remaining strips to the sides, then trim to complete the frame around the background fabric.

8 From the white fabric, cut two strips that are 1 inch (2.5 cm) x the width of the fabric and stitch the strips around the outside edge as in step 7.

9 From the dark background fabric, cut one strip that is 2¾ inches (7 cm) wide and one strip that is 1¾ inches (4.4 cm) wide, both x the width of the fabric. Cut each strip in half lengthwise, then stitch the narrow strips to the top and bottom edges of the quilt top and the wider strips to the sides. Square up the quilt top.

10 Make a quilt sandwich of the backing, batting, and quilt top, then pin or baste all layers in place. Quilt as desired. The sample shows machine stitching along the seams of the borders and hand sewing on the background fabric and around the border.

11 Using scraps, cut strips that measure 2 inches (5.1 cm) wide and 5 to 9 inches (12.7 to 22.9 cm) long. Stitch the strips end-to-end to make approximately 3 yards (2.75 m) of binding. Attach the binding to the quilt (page 17).

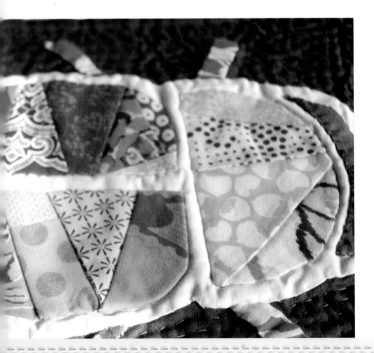

crazy quilt

Vintage textured fabrics, sewn together crazy-quilt-style, make a memory quilt with a story to tell.

handmade by **KATHERINE "SUESUE" BOLLINGER**

fabric & such

- 1 piece of lightweight muslin or sheeting for foundation, sized to your preference
- 1 piece of lightweight batting, sized to the foundation piece
- Scraps of fabric, with clean edges, at least 2 to 3 inches (5.1 to 7.6 cm) wide
- Embroidery floss, charms, buttons, lace, ribbon, or other embellishments
- 1 piece of backing fabric, sized to the foundation piece
- 1 fat quarter (45.7 x 55.9 cm) of binding fabric

tools

Basic Patchwork Kit (page 8)

finished size

21¾ x 19 inches (55.2 x 48.3 cm)

seam allowance

¼ inch (6 mm)

get started

1 Lay the foundation fabric on top of the batting, right side facing up.

2 Using the sample as a guide and the foundation piecing method (page 11), cut a five-sided polygon and pin it in the middle of the foundation fabric. Cut another piece of scrap fabric and lay it on one edge of the polygon. Sew a decorative stitch along the edge where they meet. Trim to make a straight edge (A).

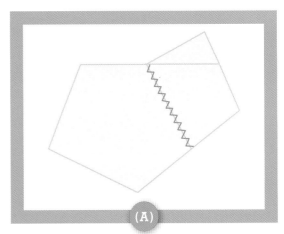

(A)

3 Cut a third piece of scrap fabric and overlap one edge over both pieces. Sew a different decorative stitch along that edge (B). As you stitch your pieces, raise each one up and trim the fabric beneath to reduce bulk.

4 Continue in this manner around the polygon, using different scraps, shapes, and decorative stitches as you go. Your strips will vary in length depending on the angle you lay them. If you don't want too long a strip, simply sew two different fabrics together with a decorative stitch and add it as one piece. Add strips at each edge to create a border.

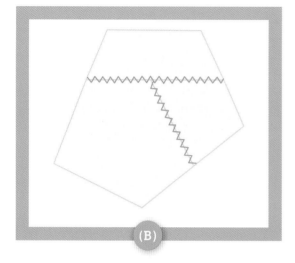

(B)

5 When the quilt top block is as large as you like, baste the edges together with a zigzag stitch. Now is the time to add embellishments, such as embroidery, charms, buttons, lace, and ribbon. If you simply zigzagged the pieces down, you may want to add lots of embroidery.

6 When complete, make a quilt sandwich of the backing, batting, and quilt top, then pin or baste all layers in place. Square up the edges.

7 Make bias strips from the binding fabric and bind the quilt (page 17).

making it your own

The simple beauty of this project, and a crazy quilt in general, is that it's so easy to personalize. Try these ideas:

- Use the textured fabrics with cotton thread and dye the finished quilt.
- Use velvet or satin fabrics for added dimension.
- Use scraps from clothes you've made for your children.
- Stitch lots of blocks with decorative stitches directly onto a finished tablecloth or sheet to make a large quilt.

catherine wheel

Ready for an exercise in precise paper piecing and top-notch organization? You can do it...pinky promise!

handmade by BRIONI GREENBERG

---

fabric & such

1 jelly roll with bright colors or 20 strips of fabric in graduating colors, each 2½ inches (6.4 cm) x the width of the fabric

1 piece of backing fabric, at least 26 inches square (66 cm)

1 piece of batting, 26 inches square (66 cm)

1 piece of binding fabric, 4 inches (10.2 cm) x the width of fabric

tools

Basic Patchwork Kit (page 8)

Templates (page 125)

Paper for paper piecing

Glue stick

Spray starch (optional)

Free motion/darning sewing machine foot (optional)

finished size

23 inches (58.4 cm) in diameter

seam allowance

¼ inch (6 mm) unless otherwise noted

---

get started

1 Enlarge and cut out the wedge templates. You need eight of each wedge type (16 in total) to complete the project. Cut the wedges into individual pieces—except 1A and 2A, leave these as one piece for foundation piecing and set aside.

2 Decide on your color scheme. Choose four groups of colors from the fabric strips that graduate from light to dark. You will need five strips in each group. Two groups will be used for each wedge to ensure all the colors coordinate nicely.

> **Tip** *Label your strips to match the template numbers so you remember which color is being used for which strip and to save confusion when cutting your fabric.*

3 To prepare your fabric pieces, use the glue stick to adhere the paper pieces onto the wrong side of the fabric strips, with the piece numbers facing you. The template pieces do not include the ¼ inch (6 mm) seam allowance. Cut out each template piece from the fabric, including the seam allowance.

4 For all the pieces except 1A and 2A and using the English paper piecing method (page 10), fold the seam allowance to the paper side and baste the allowance to the paper (A). Using the numbers on the pieces as a guide, whip stitch the edges of the shapes together to create the individual strips that will later be used to construct the wedge.

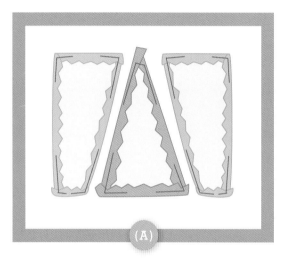

(A)

5 For paper pieces 1A and 2A, switch to foundation piecing (page 11) with the paper templates as follows:

- Cut three fabric pieces (two sides and one center) at approximately 1½ inch (3.8 cm) wide.

- Turn the paper piece face down so that the lines are on the bottom.

- Lay one of the side fabric pieces onto the paper so that the fabric completely covers the background area. Holding it to the light will help you position it correctly.

- Place a piece of fabric for the center triangle over the first piece of fabric and line up the edges (B).

- Reduce the stitch length on your sewing machine, turn over the work and sew down the stitch line (C).

- Press the pieces open.

- Trim away the seam allowance to approximately ⅛ inch (3 mm).

- Using the same method, attach the other side piece (D and E).

- Trim away the seam allowance to approximately ⅛ inch (3 mm).

- To complete the point, lay the fabric (right side together) over the section you just pieced so the top edges line up. Sew across the wedge at the stitch line and press the piece open (F).

- Wrap the fabric around the paper and baste, as you would in the English paper piecing method (G).

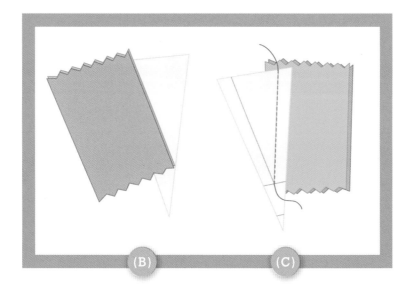

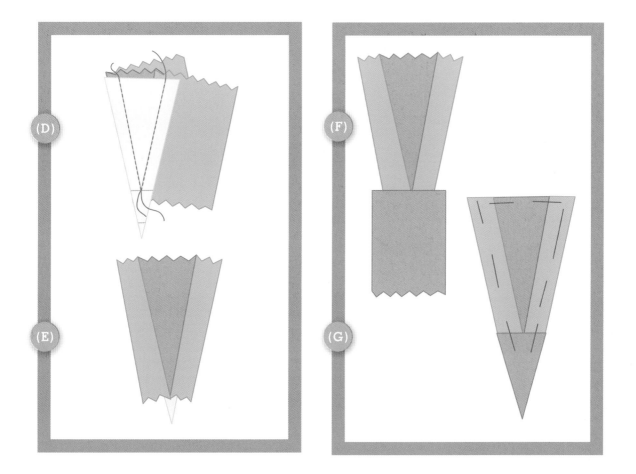

6 Assemble the wedges following these instructions:

- Starting at one end of the wedge, place the pieces (or rows) right sides together ensuring that the edges are lined up as accurately as possible, and whip stitch them together.

- Continue to add rows until you've completed the wedge.

- Continue until you have completed all 16 wedges. Press with a hot iron and ensure that the shapes of the wedges do not distort.

> **Tip** *You could enlarge and copy another template sheet and lay each complete wedge onto it to ensure that the wedges are straight.*

7 Join the completed wedges together following these instructions:

- On all wedges, fold each strip in half horizontally, aligning the top and bottom stitch lines of each row. This ensures that the fold is down the very center of the strip.

- Press lightly or finger press so that a crease is formed halfway down each strip. This is to help you with placement of the wedges when sewing them all together to complete the quilt top.

- Place two wedges right sides together, ensuring that the pressed crease of one wedge lines up with the stitching lines of the other, and the ends of the wedges match up. Whip stitch the two wedges together.

- Sew the wedges into groups of four so that you have four quarter circles.

- Sew the quarters together.

- Press well with a hot iron.

8 Add the center following these instructions:

- Cut out one octagon template.

- Adhere the template onto the back of your chosen fabric and cut around it, leaving ¼ inch (6 mm) of fabric all the way around the paper template.

- Fold the fabric to the back of the paper and baste in place.

- Press the octagon with a hot iron so that the edges of the shape are nice and crisp; use a little spray starch if needed.

- Remove the basting thread and carefully remove the paper template.

- Pin the octagon to the center of the quilt top, making sure that the shape covers all the ends of the points, and appliqué in place.

9 Remove all the papers by clipping the threads and gently easing the papers out.

10 Unfold the seam allowance around the outside edge and press open.

11 Make a quilt sandwich of the backing, batting, and quilt top, then pin baste. Using coordinating thread, pebble quilt (page 16) the background of all the type 2 wedges, the inside of the triangles on the type 1 wedges, and the center octagon and the spokes that come off it.

12 Trim the quilt straight across the top of every wedge using your ruler and rotary cutter.

13 Cut and scrap piece the binding fabric to make a bias strip at least 2 x 76 inches (5.1 x 193 cm) and bind the quilt (page 17). You may need to add a small miter at each corner of the wedges.

chair quilt

A free-pieced chair, prairie points, plus signs, and a pretty perched birdie—there's so much to love!

handmade by **LUCINDA JONES**

fabric & such

- ½ yard (.5 m) total of orange fabric in prints and solid shades
- ½ yard (.5 m) total of aqua fabric in prints and solid shades
- ½ yard (.5 m) total of white fabric
- Embroidery floss or perle cotton for the bird beak, wing, and legs
- 1 piece of backing fabric, 20 x 24 inches (50.8 x 61 cm)
- 1 piece of lightweight batting, 25 inches square (63.5 cm)
- 1 fat quarter (45.7 x 55.9 cm) of binding fabric, or fabric scraps for binding strips
- Quilting weight thread or perle cotton for top quilting

tools

Basic Patchwork Kit (page 8)

Templates (page 120)

Paper for paper piecing

finished size

21½ x 17½ inches (54.6 x 44.5 cm), excluding triangle edging

seam allowance

¼ inch (6 mm)

notes:

• *The background fabrics (behind the chair) can be all the same fabric or a random assortment. They can be large pieces or pieced from 2 or more fabrics.*

• *There should be enough contrast between the chair fabrics and the background to make the chair stand out and not be "lost".*

get started

1 To make the chair top, cut and lay out the pieces as follows, using the diagram (A) and the dimensions below as a guide. Stitch each vertical section first, and square off to the correct width and height. Then stitch the vertical sections together from left to right.

- From orange fabric, cut:
  Piece A: 3 x 1¾ inches (7.6 x 4.4 cm)
  Pieces B and C: 3 x ¾ inches (7.6 x 1.9 cm)
  Pieces J and K: 1½ x 6 inches (3.8 x 15.2 cm)

- From aqua fabrics, cut:
  Piece D: 3 x 2¾ inches (7.6 x 7 cm)
  Piece E: 3 x 1½ inches (7.6 x 3.8 cm)
  Piece F: 3 x 1¼ inches (7.6 x 3.2 cm)
  Piece G: 3 x 2 inches (7.6 x 5.1 cm)
  Pieces H and I: 1½ x 2 inches (3.8 x 5.1 cm)
  Piece L: 2¾ x 7 inches (7 x 17.8 cm)
  Piece M: 3½ x 7 inches (8.9 x 17.8 cm)

2 To create the bird, enlarge the template and use it to cut out your fabric pieces. Make sure there is enough fabric for the seam allowance on all outside edges. Use the numbers on the template as follows:

- Foundation paper piece (page 11) 1 and 2 (the bird body) with fabric colors that contrast nicely with the aqua fabric for the chair seat.

- Add pieces 3, 4, and 5, using scraps of aqua.

- Piece 6, 7, and 8 separately; use bird colors for 6 (the bird tail) and aqua scraps for 7 and 8.

- Stitch the 6, 7, and 8 piece to the main block (at the seam indicated).

- Add 9 and 10 last, both from aqua.

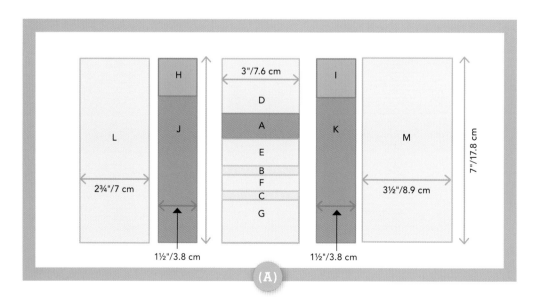

3 To make the chair seat (B):

- From aqua, cut a piece that measures at least 6 inches square (15.2 cm) for piece O; you will reshape it later.

- From a lighter background fabric, cut squares for pieces N and P that each measure at least 5 inches square (12.7 cm).

- Square up the pieced bird section, allowing for the seam allowance on all sides. Cut the piece O square in half vertically and sew the pieced bird between the two halves, aligning the bottom of the bird block with the bottom of the fabric. Lightly press. This is the center seat piece.

- Place the center seat piece below the pieced chair top. Using a ruler and rotary cutter, trim the side edges of the center seat to the angles of your choice (C). Make sure to leave ¼ inch (6 mm) at the edges for the seam allowance.

- With all pieces right side up, overlap the edges of the center seat and side pieces N and P. Cut the side pieces to match the angles on both sides of the seat (D). Stitch pieces N and P to the seat as shown, and use a rotary cutter to straighten the top and bottom edges.

- To decide the height of the seat before sewing, again place the chair top section on top of the pieced seat section and use a ruler to mark where to cut. For piece R cut a strip that measures 1 inch (2.5 cm) x the width of the chair seat bottom plus ¼-inch (6 mm) seam allowance on both ends. (Hint: For piece R use a fabric that is a lighter shade than the seat bottom so that the chair will

appear to have dimension.) Cut pieces Q and S from background fabric to measure at least 1 x 3 inches (2.5 x 7.6 cm).

- Stitch pieces Q and S to the ends of piece R. Use a rotary cutter to straighten the top of this section and the bottom of the chair seat section, then stitch the two sections together.

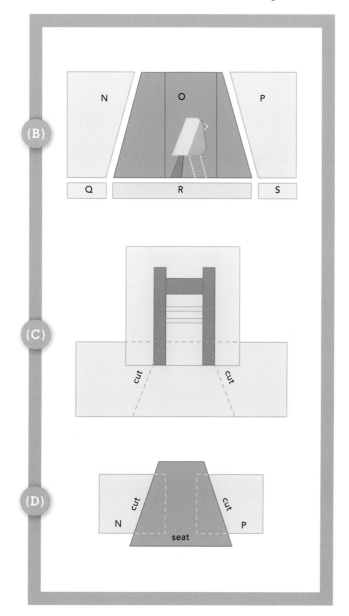

4 Make 12 to 14 plus-sign blocks for the "floor" below the chair. Start by cutting strips that measure 1 inch (2.5 cm) wide from assorted fabrics and from the white fabric. To make each block:

- Stitch together lengthwise a white strip, color strip, and another white strip. If the pieced strips are of uneven lengths, trim the block, then press (E).

- Cut apart the three sewn strips as shown. The cut does not have to be centered; cut anywhere you like for off-center plus signs.

- Add a strip of fabric between the cut sections and stitch together.

- Cut the finished piece to 2½ inches (6.4 cm) wide x various lengths.

5 To make the chair leg section, cut and lay out the pieces as follows, using the diagram (F) and dimensions below as a guide.

- From a light blue background fabric, cut:
  Piece T: 3¼ inch (8.3 cm) square
  Piece Y: 1¾ x 3¼ inch (4.4 x 8.3 cm)
  Piece Z: 2¼ x 3¼ inch (5.7 x 8.3 cm)

- Cut the back chair legs (U and V) from one of your darker orange fabrics to show the back legs in shadow: 1¼ x 3¼ inches (3.2 x 8.3 cm) each.

- From lighter orange fabric, cut the front chair legs (W and X): 1¾ x 5 inches (4.4 x 12.7 cm) each.

- Lay out the pieces as shown in diagram (F), trimming and fitting plus sign blocks as needed. Taking seam allowances into consideration, check that the chair legs line up underneath the chair seat.

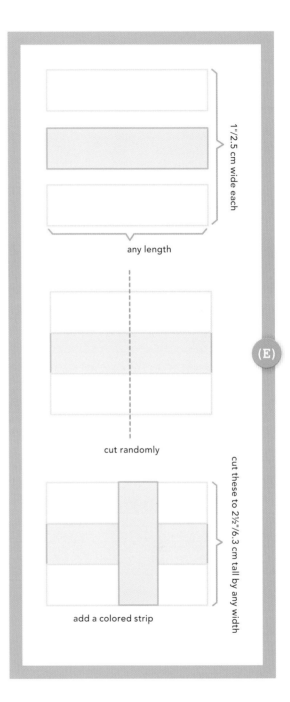

1"/2.5 cm wide each

any length

cut randomly

add a colored strip

cut these to 2½"/6.3 cm tall by any width

(E)

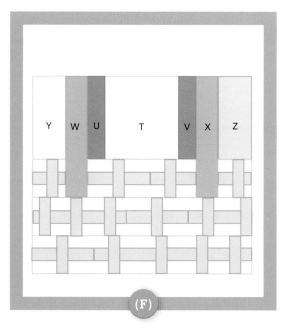

(F)

7 To make the vertical band of triangles (called Flying Geese):

- Cut 3½-inch squares (8.9 cm) from 11 or 12 dark-colored fabrics.

- Cut these squares in half diagonally, corner to corner.

- Stitch light-colored background fabrics to both sides of these triangles.

- Square up the edges and stitch the blocks together in one long strip approximately the height of the pieced chair block. You can always add a background strip to the top of the chair section (as shown in the sample) to match up the columns.

- Press and square up the side edges of this strip.

8 From the aqua fabric (or a fabric color of your choice), cut two sashing strips that each measure 2 to 2¾ inches (5.1 to 7 cm) x the height of the pieced chair block. Stitch a sashing strip to each side of the Flying Geese, then press. Stitch this section to the side of the pieced chair block.

9 Embroider the bird beak, legs, and wing as desired. Add French knots or any other embroidery stitches as you like.

10 To make the triangle edging, enlarge and cut out the triangle template.

- Use the template to cut seven triangles from the same fabric as the sashing, seven from the backing fabric, and seven from the batting.

- Pin two different-colored triangles together, right sides facing, with a batting triangle on the bottom. Stitch two edges,

- To sew the block, start by stitching a plus sign to the bottom of piece Y. Press the seam, then stitch to the long side of W. Set aside.

- Stitch pieces U, T, and V along the sides. Press and trim. Add a row of plus sign blocks below. Press and set aside.

- Stitch a plus sign block to the bottom of piece Z. Press, then stitch to the side of X.

- Square up the pieces as needed and stitch the three pieced sections together.

- Stitch two rows of plus signs together to match the width of the upper pieced section, and stitch to the bottom edge. Press and straighten all four sides.

6 Stitch together the pieced sections for the chair top, chair seat, and chair legs. Press and square up the outer edges.

leaving the bottom edge open. Repeat with the remaining triangle pieces.

■ Trim the seams and the tip of each stitched triangle. Turn right side out and press lightly.

11 For the final assembly:

■ Lay the batting (slightly larger than the backing or quilt top) on a flat surface.

■ Center the quilt top, right side facing up, on the batting.

■ Position the triangles, right side facing down (toward the quilt top), down the chair side of the quilt, matching raw edges. As you pin, overlap the sides of the triangles about ¼ inch (6 mm) from the bottom raw edge. When the seam is stitched, it should intersect where the triangles overlap.

■ Add the quilt backing last, right side facing down.

■ Stitch the side where the triangles are pinned. Trim the batting and seam allowance, and flip the backing over to the back. The triangles should now be pointing out the left side of the quilt. Lightly press the quilt and baste the layers flat.

■ Quilt by machine or by hand as desired.

12 Cut strips from the binding fabric and bind the three remaining edges of the quilt (page 17).

ticker tape quilt

Quilt-iqué? Appli-quilt? Whatever you call it, this quilt is the reason that you keep all of those fabric tidbits and scraps!

handmade by **CATHY GAUBERT**

fabric & such

1 piece of cotton or linen fabric for background, 24 x 19 inches (61 x 48.3 cm)

Scraps of assorted fabric, 1 to 3 x 1½ to 6 inches (2.5 to 7.6 x 3.8 to 15.2 cm)

1 piece of backing fabric, 24 x 19 inches (61 x 48.3 cm)

1 piece of batting, 25 x 20 inches (63.5 x 50.8 cm)

1 fat quarter (45.7 x 55.9 cm) of binding fabric

tools

Basic Patchwork Kit (page 8)

Washable glue stick, or other fabric adhesive

finished size

24 x 19 inches (61 x 48.3 cm)

seam allowance

¼ inch (6 mm)

get started

1 Fold the background fabric in half widthwise, then press. Open the fabric and fold it in the other direction. Press again. The quadrants will help you place your scrap fabrics in an orderly manner.

2 Choose a scrap fabric for a focal point of the quilt, if desired. Then group the remaining scraps into color families. Square up any edges as needed as you place and arrange them on the background.

3 After you have arranged (and rearranged!) your fabric pieces into a design you like, use a gluestick (or a preferred fabric adhesive) to adhere each piece to the background. It helps to start in the center and work your way outward.

4 Now for the quilting.

- Make a quilt sandwich of the backing, batting, and quilt top, then pin all layers in place.

- Machine quilt vertical and horizontal lines about ½ inch (1.3 cm) apart. Start in the middle of the quilt and work your way toward the edges. By stitching both vertically and horizontally, the edges of the fabric scraps should be secured nicely. At this point, you can go back and add more straight line quilting at varying intervals between the previously quilted lines.

5 Cut strips from the binding fabric and bind the quilt (page 17).

diamond lattice

Look through the latticework to see your favorite fabrics stitched up into patchwork diamonds.

handmade by PENNY LAYMAN

fabric & such

Scraps of assorted fabric

½ yard (.5 m) of white fabric, for sashing and border

Size 3 cotton crochet thread in two colors

1 piece of batting, 22 x 25 inches (55.9 x 63.5 cm)

1 piece of fabric for backing, 22 x 25 inches (55.9 x 63.5 cm)

3 yards (2.75 m) of binding

tools

Basic Patchwork Kit (page 8)

Template (page 121)

finished size

23 x 19½ inches (58.4 x 49.5 cm)

seam allowance

¼ inch (6 mm) unless otherwise noted

get started

1 Enlarge and cut out the template. For each of the 12 diamonds needed, choose three fabric scraps that appeal to you when placed next to each other. The pieces should be long and wide enough, when sewn together, to cut a diamond with the template.

2 For each diamond, stitch the three scraps together, straightening the edges (if necessary) before piecing. Press the pieced fabric with both seams in the same direction.

3 Using the template, cut a diamond from each of the pieced fabrics, for a total of 12 diamonds.

4 To make the diamond fragments that fill out the edges of the quilt, cut the following:

- Cut two of the diamonds in half from tip to tip across the width of the diamonds.

- Cut one diamond in half from tip to tip down the length of the diamond.

- Cut one diamond into quarters, from tip to tip lengthwise and then from tip to tip widthwise.

5 From the white fabric, cut nine sashing strips that each measure 1¾ inches (4.4 cm) x the fabric width.

6 Arrange the diamonds in a pleasing manner according to the diagram (A), and lay strips between the diamonds. Cut the strips to fit in one direction, leaving them long in the other direction.

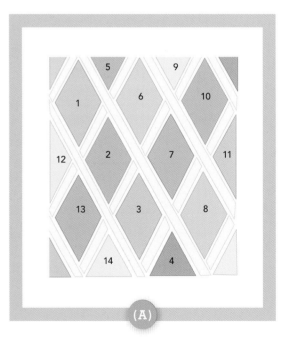

(A)

7 Sew the diamonds together in strips, as follows:

- Stitch a strip of sashing to the bottom right edge of diamonds 1, 2, and 3. Press and trim the ends of the strips on a diagonal as needed to line them up with the diamonds.

- Stitch the upper left edge of each of these diamonds to the bottom of the adjacent sashing. Press and trim.

- Stitch diamond 4 to the adjacent sashing below diamond 3. Press and trim. Do not stitch the corner piece above diamond 1.

- Assemble the row with diamonds 5, 6, 7, and 8 in the same way, leaving off the corner below diamond 8.

- Assemble the row with diamonds 9, 10, and 11 in the same way.

- Assemble the row with diamonds 12, 13, and 14 in the same way.

- Stitch each pieced row to the adjacent long strips. Add the unsewn corners last. Press and trim.

8 Stitch long strips, about 1¾ inches (4.4 cm) wide, to the quilt top to make a border, starting with the right edge, then the bottom, then the left edge, then the top edge. Press and square up the edges.

9 Make a quilt sandwich of the backing, batting, and quilt top, then pin securely every 3 to 5 inches (7.6 to 12.7 cm). Quilt using a straight stitch through the sashing only, randomly placing the stitches and the color of thread used. Make sure to sew at least one line (and up to three lines) of quilting down each section of sashing.

10 Bind the quilt (page 17).

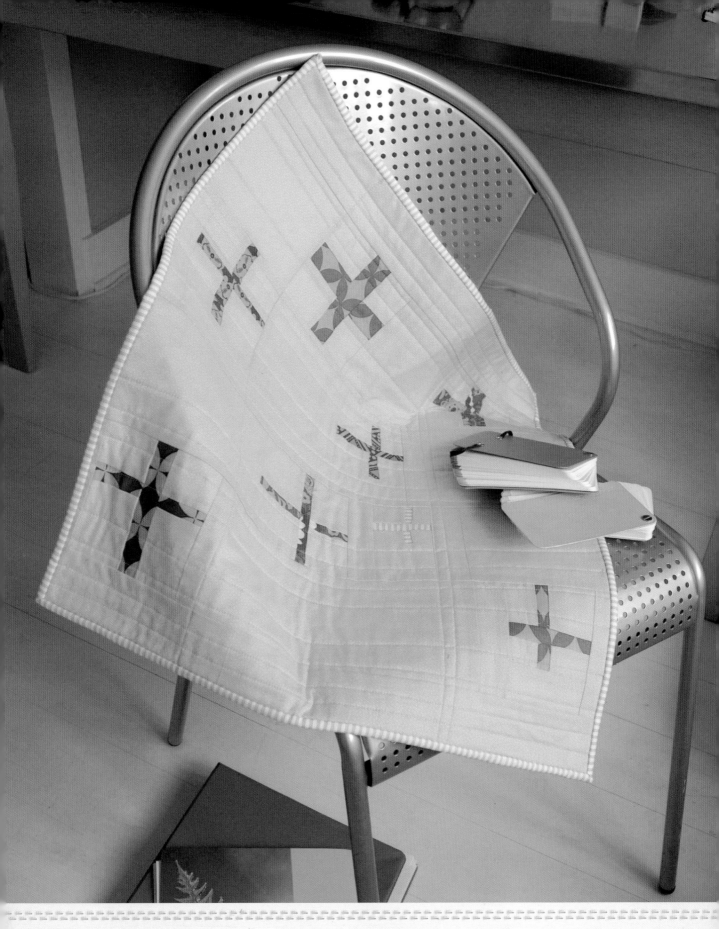

A+ doll quilt

Impromptu piecing + your favorite color scheme = an excellent grade from all of your dollies!

handmade by CATHY GAUBERT

get started

1 With the rotary cutter, cut eight 5-inch squares (12.7 cm) from the background fabric. For each square, slice once vertically and once horizontally, dividing the square into four pieces. (No rulers here—just trust yourself, and go for it!) After cutting, place the pieces back together into squares and set aside. (This is a different method for creating plus signs than that used on page 58. Choose whichever method works best for you.)

2 Snip off two 6-inch (15.2 cm) lengths from the scrap fabrics for each plus that you want to make. Snip one of each pair of strips in half, giving you one 6-inch (15.2 cm) strip and two 3-inch (7.6 cm) strips for each plus. The quilt shown uses eight sets of strips.

3 Pick up one of the squares that you cut into four pieces, and lay them out in front of you (labeled

A, B, C, and D in A). Choose a complimentary set of fabric scrap strips, and stitch one of the short strips between A and B (B) and the remaining short strip between C and D (C). If necessary, snip the ends of the fabric strips flush with the sides. Press the seams. Stitch the long fabric scrap strip between the stitched rows, as shown. Repeat this process to make the remaining plus blocks.

4 With your rotary cutter and ruler:

- Trim five blocks to 5 inches square (12.7 cm).

- Trim two blocks to 4 inches square (10.2 cm).

- Trim one to 3 inches square (7.6 cm).

Tip Line up the plus with the ruler's edge for a more centered block, or rotate the plus either left or right to make a wonkier block.

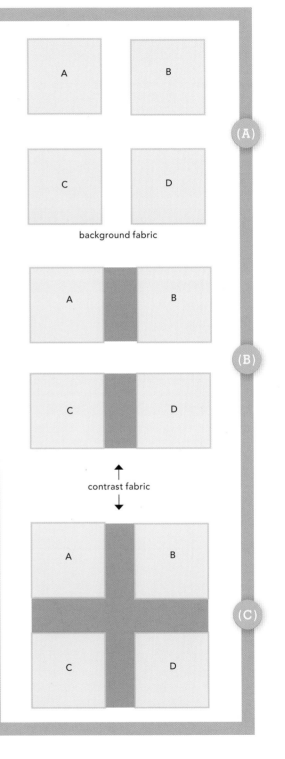

background fabric

contrast fabric

(A)

(B)

(C)

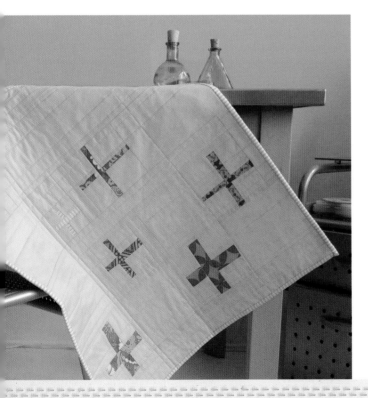

5 To make all of the squares the same size:

- Cut and stitch two strips of background fabric— each 2 inches (5.1 cm) wide—to the 4-inch (10.2 cm) blocks: one strip on the side and one strip on the bottom (D).

- To the 3-inch (7.6 cm) block, do the same, using strips 3 inches (7.6 cm) wide.

- Trim all squares to 5 inches (12.7 cm), wonk-ifiying them or not.

6 To improvise the layout, fold up the background fabric to 24 x 22 inches (61 x 55.9 cm). Scatter your plus blocks until you find a pleasing layout. If you keep them lined up in columns and rows, the piecing will be a cinch.

7 Find a good starting point, for instance the upper left-hand corner. With scissors or rotary cutter in hand, start cutting, stitching, and pressing to piece your quilt top. You can cut strips of the background fabric from selvedge to selvedge in 5-inch (12.7 cm) widths, and then cut these as needed to build your quilt top.

8 When the top is assembled, square up your quilt. Layer the quilt top, batting, and backing, and then pin or baste all layers in place. Quilt by machine or by hand in horizontal and vertical lines.

9 Cut and piece a 2½-inch-wide (6.4 cm) binding strip from your fat quarter and bind the quilt (page 17).

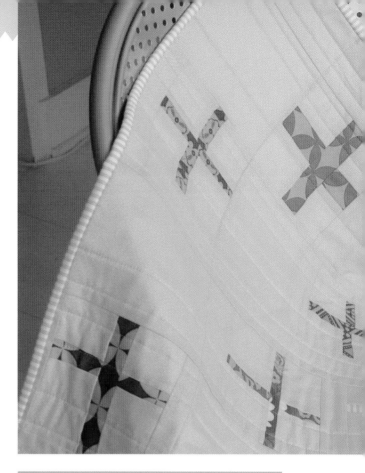

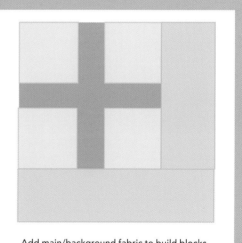

Add main/background fabric to build blocks to 5-inch squares (12.7 cm).

(D)

dream doll quilt

What's sweeter than a doll quilt? A wee doll and her quilt *on* a doll quilt!

handmade by ANEELA HOEY

fabric & such

Scraps of assorted fabrics for doll face and clothing

Embroidery floss in assorted colors

1 scrap of felt for doll hair

Scraps of brown and pink felt for teddy

Polyester fiberfill for stuffing

Scraps of fabric in assorted colors for the border squares and pockets

1 piece of backing fabric, 16 x 17 inches (40.6 x 43.2 cm)

1 piece of beige or light-colored fabric for background, 8½ x 10½-inch (21.6 x 26.7 cm)

Scraps of fusible web

1 piece of batting, 15 x 16 inches (38.1 x 40.6 cm)

60 inches (152.4 cm) of binding, 2½ inches (6.4 cm) wide

tools

Basic Patchwork Kit (page 8)

Templates (page 124)

Pencil or marker

finished size

14½ x 12¼ inches (36.8 x 31.1 cm)

seam allowance

¼ inch (6 mm) unless otherwise noted

get started

1 Enlarge the templates and cut them out.

2 To make the doll:

- Use the horizontal lines in the template as a guide for stitching fabrics together (face and nightie for a girl or face, shirt, and pants for a boy). Press. Lay the template on top of the stitched pieces, lining up the seams with the lines on the template, and cut out the doll shape.

- With the fabric right side up on top of the template, trace the features of the face and markings for buttons and collars. Using one ply of embroidery floss, stitch French knots for each eye and use a straight stitch for other facial features.

- Use the hair template to cut out the hair shape from felt and hand sew in place around the face and across the back, using a whipstitch.

- For the doll clothing, use six plies of embroidery floss to make buttons and three plies to stitch other details.

- Fold the doll in half with right sides together and stitch along the unfolded side and top edges. Cut several notches into the curved seam of the head, and then turn right side out.

- Stuff the doll and slip stitch the bottom edge closed.

3 To make the teddy, use the templates to cut out two body shapes from the brown felt and the tummy from the pink felt. As before, use the template as a guide for facial features.

- Use two plies of floss to make a French knot for each eye, and to trace the arm and leg outlines with a backstitch.

- Use four plies of floss to make a French knot for the nose and one ply of floss to backstitch the mouth.

- Stitch other details, as desired, for ears and around the tummy.

- Pin the teddy's front and back shapes together with wrong sides facing. Stitch the outer edges together two-thirds of the way around, using one ply of floss in blanket stitch. Stuff the teddy lightly, then finish using blanket stitching around the edge.

4 To make the doll's quilt:

- Cut twenty 1½-inch squares (3.8 cm) from assorted scrap fabrics.

- Make 20 half-square triangles by pinning together two squares of different colors, right sides facing. On the wrong side of one of the squares, draw a diagonal line from the top left corner to the bottom right corner. Stitch a scant ¼ inch (6 mm) seam on both sides of the marked line. Cut along the drawn line and press the seams open.

- Lay out the quilt pocket in rows of four squares across and five squares down. Stitch the squares together in rows and press. Then stitch the rows together.

- Cut a piece of backing fabric the same size as the stitched quilt. Pin with right sides together and stitch along three of the sides. Turn right side out and slip stitch the remaining side closed.

5 To make the teddy's quilt:

- Cut four 1½-inch squares (3.8 cm) from assorted scrap fabrics.

- Lay out the squares in two rows of two squares each. Stitch the squares together in rows and press. Then stitch the rows together.

- Cut and attach a piece of backing fabric in the same way as in step 4.

6 To make the background for the quilt top:

- Cut twenty-two 2½-inch squares (6.4 cm) from assorted scrap fabrics for the border.

- Stitch together five of the squares to form a strip. Repeat with another five squares to make a second strip. Press seams open.

- Stitch these strips to the 10½-inch (26.7 cm) sides of the beige background fabric. Press seams open.

- Stitch together the remaining 2½-inch (6.4 cm) squares into two strips of six squares each. Stitch these two strips to the top and bottom edges of the beige fabric background. Press the seams open.

fox stuffy

Who doesn't love a super-cute fox stuffy? Good answer! To make him, you'll need to grab a few felt scraps in orange and white. Using the templates on page 124, cut two fox body shapes and one head shape from orange felt. Cut out tummy and feet shapes from white felt. As before, mark the position of the face and body features.

1 Use one ply of embroidery floss to stitch the facial features, except for the nose. Use three plies of floss to stitch the nose with a single straight stitch.

2 Using one ply of orange floss and a running stitch, sew the head piece onto one of the body pieces.

3 Stitch the tummy, feet, and hands in place with one ply of white floss.

4 Use one ply of brown floss to stitch the middle line between the fox's legs and the edges of each arm in back stitch.

5 Pin the front body piece to the back piece, wrong sides facing, and stitch together in the same way as the teddy, using one ply of orange floss in blanket stitch.

7 To complete the center design:

■ Select scrap fabric for the clouds and press scraps of fusible web onto the back sides, following the manufacturer's instructions. Draw three cloud shapes onto the paper side of the web and cut out the shapes.

■ Lay out the clouds and the quilts, with the doll and teddy in place, to see how the design looks. When you are satisfied with the arrangement, pin the clouds and quilts in place.

■ Peel off the paper backing from the clouds and iron them into position. Hand sew the edges with a running stitch.

■ Use a slip stitch to attach the side and bottom edges of the quilts. Leave the top edges unstitched so that the doll and teddy can be slipped in and out.

8 Make a quilt sandwich of the backing, batting, and quilt top, then pin or baste all layers in place. Using a marker or a faint pencil, mark the center point of each of the four sides. With the aid of a long ruler, draw lines connecting each of the points together to make a diamond shape. Machine quilt on these lines. Quilt additional parallel lines ½ inch (1.3 cm) away from the first lines, going out toward the corners of the quilt.

9 Square up the quilt, and then bind it (page 17).

home

Simple strip piecing in bright, beautiful solids, sweet embroidery, and a charming appliquéd house come together perfectly to welcome you home.

handmade by AMY PROFF LYONS

fabric & such

7 fat quarters (45.7 x 55.9 cm) of fabric (see Notes)

Scraps of fabric in assorted colors

Lightweight fusible web

Embroidery floss in assorted colors

2 fat quarters (45.7 x 55.9 cm) or ½ yard (.5 m) of backing fabric

1 piece of batting, 22 x 24 inches (55.9 x 61 cm)

tools

Basic Patchwork Kit (page 8)

Templates (page 125)

Walking foot attachment (optional)

finished size

22 x 19¼ inches (55.9 x 48.9 cm)

seam allowance

½ inch (1.3 cm)

note: *To achieve the look of this quilt, choose fat quarters and scraps that are all solid colors rather than prints. For clarity, the colors used in the quilt are often listed in the instructions, but freely choose your own. Four of the fat quarters will be stitched together in strips to form the horizontal bands in the background; these colors will be the primary palette of the quilt, so choose your colors with this in mind.*

get started

1 To make the strips for the background, press the four coordinating fat quarters you have selected. Use a rotary cutter and quilting ruler to cut six strips that measure 2 x 22 inches (5.1 x 55.9 cm) from each of the four colors. This will give you plenty of extra for cutting and piecing. Set the strips aside.

2 For the panel behind the bird and house, cut the following two rectangles from your scraps and then set them aside:

- For the sky (aqua or light blue): 7 x 18 inches (17.8 x 45.7 cm)

- For the grass (green): 7 x 5 inches (17.8 x 12.7 cm)

3 Enlarge and cut out the templates. Select which fabrics to use for the three appliqués and also for the pieces listed below. Press fusible web onto the back of each piece, following the manufacturer's instructions. On the paper backing, trace the appliqués and draw the other pieces to size. Cut them out.

- House (white): 4 x 8½ inches (10.2 x 21.6 cm)

- House door (red): 2 x 3½ inches (5.1 x 8.9 cm)

- Two windows (dark aqua): 2 x 1 inch (5.1 x 2.5 cm)

Tip If your machine allows it, set the needle to end in the down position while "drawing" around each appliquéd piece. It will be easier to turn corners or see where a stitch needs to end.

4 Peel away the adhesive backing and fuse the pieces onto the "sky" panel as follows:

- Center the house piece with the bottom edge of the house flush with the bottom edge of the panel.

- Center the door on the house piece with the bottom edges flush.

- Position the roof piece on top of the house with the scallops of the roof overhanging the house by ½ inch (1.3 cm).

- Center the windows evenly between the top of the door and the roof scallops. If you like, use a disappearing ink fabric marker to draw lines for windowpanes.

- Center the bird 1 inch (2.5 cm) above the house, leaving room for legs. Draw two legs from the bird to the rooftop.

- Center the sun piece on the panel with the flat edge flush with the top edge of the panel.

5 With contrasting thread in your sewing machine, stitch around each appliquéd piece and along the bird legs. Pull all loose threads to the back of the panel and secure them with knots. Pin the bottom of the sky panel to the grass piece, right sides together, and stitch. Press seams open.

6 The panels to the left and right of the bird panel are made with the strips you cut in step 1, with random squares pieced into those strips. It will take 22 strips from top to bottom to match the height of the bird panel. For a balanced background, decide on the order of the four colors (for instance: light green, dark green, dark aqua, and light aqua) and use that order for each set of horizontal strips. Here are the essentials for how generating your own variation on the design (**A**). Keep in mind that the seam allowance is ½ inch (1.3 cm).

- The smallest squares (purple, yellow, red, and pink) measure 2 inches square (5.1 cm) and fit nicely into the 2-inch-wide (5.1 cm) strips.

- Medium-size squares measure 3 inches square (7.6 cm) and fit with two strips stitched together. The yellow "home" rectangle measures 4¾ x 3 inches (12 x 7.6 cm).

- The largest squares (blue and orange), in which the birds are embroidered, are 4 inches square (10.2 cm) and fit with three strips stitched together.

- Lay out the strips in order, top to bottom, for both sides of the quilt. The total length of the strips on the left side of the quilt is 11 inches (27.9 cm); on the right the strips measure 4 inches (10.2 cm) long. Start with strips a couple of inches longer than specified to allow for piecing.

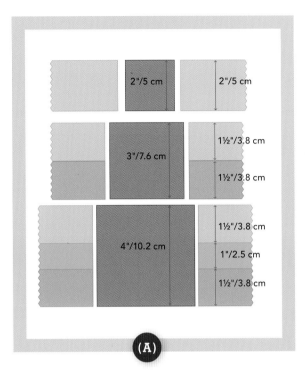

(A)

- Lay each square on top of the strip where you'd like for it to go. When you're satisfied with the arrangement, cut and piece each strip as needed, working your way down to the bottom. As you stitch strips together, press the seams each time, always in the same direction.

7 You now have three panels: the left side of the quilt, the bird appliqué panel, and the right side. Square up all three sections as needed. Pin the pieces, right sides together, on the long sides. See if you can match up the fourth seam from the bottom (on the stripped panels) with the seam between the sky and grass (on the center panel). Stitch the sides and press the seams away from the bird panel.

8 Center the quilt top on the batting and pin baste the layers together. Mark the sections you want to embroider:

- Use your fabric marker to draw hatch marks on the grass panel and roof. Also draw rays for the sun.

- Use the templates to transfer the embroidery patterns for the small birds.

9 To embroider, use three strands of floss and stitch as you like. The quilt shown was stitched as follows:

- Straight stitch the hatch marks.

- Create the sun rays by alternating between backstitch and rows of French knots.

- Create the small birds a backstitch, with French knots for the eyes.

a little back story

The designer carried the homelike theme onto the back of the quilt, using an appliquéd house as the perfect little label.

10 To assemble the quilt, sew the fat quarters of backing fabric together and make a quilt sandwich of the backing, batting, and quilt top, then pin or baste all layers in place. Use a walking foot, if you have one, to stitch in the ditch on either side of the appliqué panel. Once the panel is secured, quilt as desired. The sample shows quilted vertical lines spaced approximately 2 inches (5.1 cm) apart.

11 Square up the quilt. Cut strips from the remaining fabric and bind the quilt (page 17).

forestopia

A fresh take on flying geese, this modern quilt is the perfect way to show off a favorite fabric line with fussy-cutting.

handmade by **JOHN Q. ADAMS**

get started

1 Cut the following pieces:

- From the theme fabric, fussy cut six squares measuring 4½ inches square (11.4 cm).

- From the striped fabrics, cut 30 rectangles measuring 2½ x 4½ inches (6.4 x 11.4 cm).

- From the polka-dot fabrics, cut 60 squares measuring 2½ inches square (6.4 cm).

- From the coordinating fabrics, cut 32 squares measuring 2½ inches square (6.4 cm).

- From the binding fabric, cut four strips measuring 2½ inches (6.4 cm) x the width of the fabric.

2 To create the units of triangles (called Flying Geese):

- Draw a diagonal pencil line from corner to corner on the back of each polka-dot square.

- Take one of the striped rectangles and align a small polka-dot square with the left corner of the rectangle, right sides together. Sew on the diagonal line (A).

- Trim off the excess seam allowance ¼ (6 mm) away from the seam line, and press the remainder toward the outer triangle.

- Repeat with another square on the opposite end. You can use the same dotted print on both sides of the rectangle for a cohesive look, or you might choose to use a more random, scrappy method.

- Repeat for all of your striped and dotted fabrics, until you have 30 Flying Geese units.

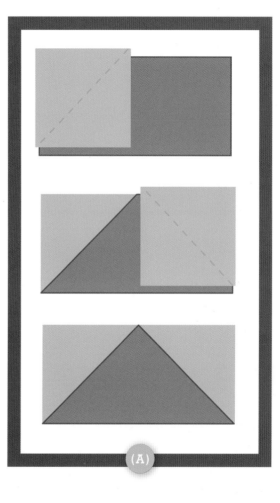

(A)

Tip *If you are comfortable chain piecing, you can sew all of the squares to one side of all of the rectangles, do all of your trimming and pressing, and then repeat for the other side of all rectangles. You can also use chain piecing to construct the four-patch units in step 4.*

3 Join the Flying Geese units into pairs by stitching together two Flying Geese units with the geese "flying" in the same direction. This will result in a 4½-inch (11.4 cm) square unit. I chose each unit to contain only one striped and one dotted fabric; however, a scrappy approach would work here, too. Repeat for all Flying Geese units, for a total of 15 squares.

4 To create four-patch units:

- From the coordinating prints, sew the 2½-inch (6.4 cm) squares together in pairs, for a total of 16 rectangles measuring 2½ x 4½ inches (6.4 x 11.4 cm).

- Sew the rectangles together again in pairs, resulting in eight 4-patch units measuring 4½ inches square (11.4 cm). Throughout this step, be conscious both of color dispersion throughout the four-patch unit and the correct placement of directional prints.

in the family

This sweet little doll quilt was passed down to my twin daughters from my wife's mother, continuing a long family tradition of passing it from generation to generation of young girls. It is quite simple in its design and construction, featuring a variation on the popular and traditional Sunbonnet Sue character. What's most important about this quilt, however, is that it obviously has been well used and loved by all that have held it. This is no art quilt—it's highly functional! It's great to see my daughters using it to cover their dolls at night, knowing that generations of women have done the same before them.

—John Adams

(B)

5 You should now have thirty 4½-inch (11.4 cm) square units, consisting of seven fussy cut squares, 15 double Flying Geese units, and eight 4-patch units. Lay out the quilt in rows of five squares across and six squares down using the layout diagram (B) as a guide. Or, because the units are all square, you can easily adjust the block layout. Feel free to change the placement of your blocks in a way that is pleasing to you.

6 Join the blocks together in rows, and then join the rows together. Press seams away from the Flying Geese units to help reduce the bulk in the seams, and press seams in alternating directions when joining the rows together.

7 Stack the quilt layers. Quilt and bind as desired (page 17).

maverick star

Quick, easy, and the perfect pick for repurposed fabric, you'll have this one made before bedtime.

handmade by CATHY GAUBERT

fabric & such

½ yard (.5 m) of cotton or linen fabric for background

9 coordinating fabrics, each at least 8 inches square (20.3 cm)

½ yard (.5 m) of backing fabric

1 piece of batting, 25 inches square (63.5 cm)

1 fat quarter (45.7 x 55.9 cm) of binding fabric

tools

Basic Patchwork Kit (page 8)

Spray starch or sizing (optional, if using linen)

finished size

23 inches (58.4 cm) square

seam allowance

¼ inch (6 mm)

get started

1 Cut eight 8-inch (20.3 cm) squares from the background fabric and set aside.

> *Tip* *If you are using linen, spray with starch or sizing and then press with steam to make the linen a bit stiffer before cutting and sewing.*

2 Cut nine 8-inch (20.3 cm) squares from the coordinating fabrics. Decide which square will be the center block of the star and set that one aside. Cut the remaining eight squares in half diagonally from corner to corner. You will need eight triangles for the star's rays (with eight triangles leftover). Arrange the rays around the center block until you are satisfied with the placement.

3 Now it's time for impromptu piecing. Your placement of the triangles on the background squares will determine how large or small the star's rays are:

- With right sides together, place the triangle on the block and stitch along the edge (**A**). Press. With your rotary cutter, slice off the extra bit of fabric that is now behind the ray.

- Pick up the next triangle and place onto the same block. You can overlap the other ray if you like (**B**). Stitch and press. Slice off any excess fabric from the back and square up with a rotary cutter and ruler.

- Repeat three more times for the remaining triangles and blocks.

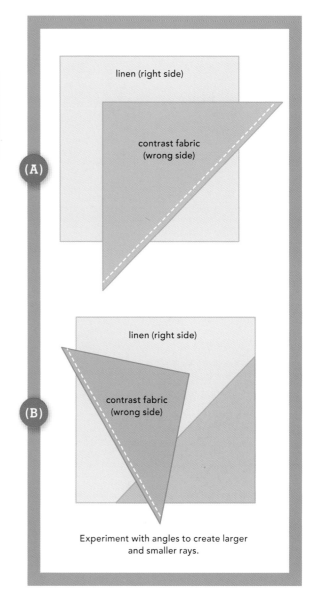

Experiment with angles to create larger and smaller rays.

4 Lay out all the blocks to form the star. You may want to do some rearranging at this point. Once you have a design you like, begin stitching blocks together into three rows, starting with the top row (C), before stitching rows 2 and 3. Press each row after stitching. Then pin together rows 1 and 2, taking care to match the seams. Stitch and press. Stitch row 3 to row 2 in the same way. Press and square up the quilt top, if needed.

5 Make a quilt sandwich of the backing, batting, and quilt top, then pin or baste all layers in place. Machine-quilt using four sets of three straight lines: horizontally, vertically, and diagonally, all running through the center of the star.

6 Cut a 2½-inch-wide (6.4 cm) binding strip from your fat quarter and bind the quilt (page 17).

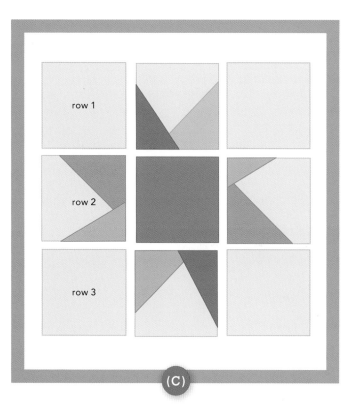

row 1

row 2

row 3

(C)

mushroom hunting for baba yaga

This story quilt tells its tale through carefully chosen fabrics and embellishments that make up Baba Yaga's enchanted forest.

handmade by **JEN OSBORN**

fabric & such

Fabric scraps in assorted colors

1 fat quarter (45.7 x 55.9 cm) of fabric for the main background

Heart and star buttons, or other embellishments

1 scrap of muslin

¾ yard (.7 m) of backing fabric

1 piece of low-loft batting, 20 x 24 inches (50.8 x 61 cm)

Scraps of red and white felt for mushrooms

tools

Basic Patchwork Kit (page 8)

Templates (page 122)

Paper for paper piecing

Fine tip fabric markers

Watercolor pencils

finished size

17½ x 22 inches (44.5 x 55.9 cm)

seam allowance

¼ inch (6 mm)

get started

1 Use the diagram and dimensions on page 92 as a guide for creating the background for the story (**A**), starting with the straight-cut pieces. The sample uses pieced fabric strips for the ground (H).

- Cut pieces A and B: 11½ x 4 inches (29.2 x 10.2 cm)

- Cut piece H: 22½ x 4 inches (57.2 x 10.2 cm)

2 For the pieces with diagonal edges, cut the pieces to the dimensions as listed below (**B**). Then follow the diagram to measure ½ inch (1.3 cm) from the sides as indicated, and cut a diagonal line from this mark to the nearest opposite corner. The sample uses pieced fabric strips for the trees (D and F) and the background fabric for pieces (C, E, and G).

- Cut piece C: 4½ x 11 inches (11.4 x 27.9 cm)

- Cut pieces D, E, and F: 3 x 11 inches (7.6 x 27.9 cm)

- Cut piece G: 13 x 11 inches (33 x 27.9 cm)

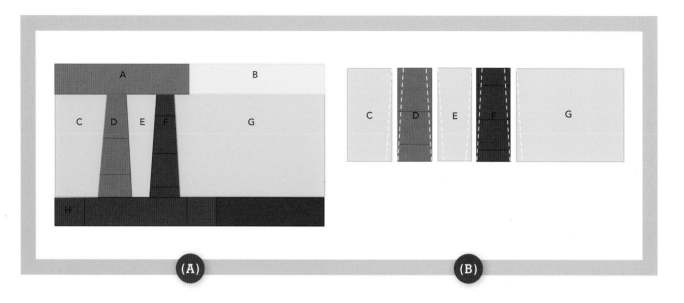

(A)

(B)

3 Stitch together the pieces of each panel as follows:

- Stitch A to B at the short ends and press the seam toward the darker fabric.

- Stitch pieces C through G, pressing the seams toward the tree pieces (D and F).

- Stitch the bottom of the AB panel to the top of the C–G panel, pressing seams toward AB.

- Stitch panel H to the bottom of the C–G panel and press the seams toward H.

Your background is now complete.

4 Create the chicken hut by stitching fabric scraps together in a wonky log cabin shape, stitching rectangular pieces together in a counterclockwise pattern until you have about a 6-inch (15.2 cm) square. Trim the edges; you can square up or tilt the square, or cut an irregular shape, as you like. Then turn under all four sides ½ inch (1.3 cm) and press.

5 Position the pieced square onto the background (piece G), leaving room for the chicken legs at the bottom and a roof on top. Machine stitch around the edges to secure.

6 Make a triangular roof from one or more fabrics pieced together, to the size you like. Once again turn under the edges and press, then stitch the roof in place. Embellish with buttons or other interesting items.

7 To complete the chicken hut, enlarge and cut out the templates for the chicken legs, then cut them from fabric scraps. Abut the top of the legs against the bottom of the house and use a tight zigzag stitch around all outer edges of the legs.

8 Enlarge the templates for Marusia and cut them out. Select fabrics for the body and scarf and use muslin fabric for the face. Cut the fabrics ¼ inch (6 mm) larger than each template for English paper piecing (page 10). Turn the seam allowance to the back of each piece and baste to the office paper. Press the pieces so they hold their shape; remove the paper.

9 Position the pieces onto the background to form Marusia's body. Turning the face piece at a slight angle gives the appearance of a scarf on her head. Use fabric markers (test them on fabric scraps first) to draw her facial features and watercolor pencils to color in the hair and cheeks.

10 Stitch on the felt scraps to form a mushroom, and draw more mushrooms directly onto the background, as you like.

11 Make a quilt sandwich of the backing, batting, and quilt top, and then pin or baste all layers in place. Quilt as desired.

12 Bind the quilt (page 17). The binding shown was made by alternating pieces of red-and-white fabrics with blue-and-white fabrics to create a striped look. To make one like it:

- Cut 70 to 80 scraps that each measure 2 x 5 inches (5.1 x 12.7 cm).

- Stitch the short sides together to make 4 strips long enough to attach to each side of the quilt.

- Pin the strips to the top and bottom edges and stitch using a 1 inch (2.5 cm) seam allowance. Then do the same on the sides.

- Press the binding to the back. You can turn under the edges and stitch them, or just stitch them flat without turning.

story time with Jen Osborn

This project is actually what I call a story quilt. Using the prints on the fabric instead of words, I've created an adaptation of what was my favorite story as a young girl: *Baba Yaga* by Ernest Small, illustrated by Blair Lent (Houghton Mifflin, 1966). Based in Russian folklore, this story is about a witch in a house on chicken legs (yes, my dear, chicken legs) that roams the darkest parts of the forest. It's said that she likes to eat bad little boys and girls, and I believed it! I'm not sure exactly what about this story so endeared it to me, but to this day I'm constantly inspired by and drawn to it. In my Baba Yaga quilt, I've depicted a scene from the story: the scared Marusia searches for things to put in Baba Yaga's pot—other than herself.

When you make your own version of this quilt, use unusual fabrics to help tell the story. Chilly snowflakes fill the sky, earthy batiks form the trees, and the treetop fabric contains leafy foliage. The ground fabrics are also earthy, with a piece that looks like roots, and an eye-catching skull and bones print fabric tell the witch's tale. The top right piece is a ghostly print in white to represent the souls of the children Baba Yaga has eaten. Spooky!

jacob's ladder

Two traditional patchwork block patterns and bold fabric choices combine to make a simply stunning modern doll quilt.

handmade by RITA HODGE, RED PEPPER QUILTS

fabric & such

¼ yard (.23 m) of dark fabric for four-patch units

¼ yard (.23 m) of light fabric for four-patch units

¼ yard (.23 m) of dark fabric for half-square triangles

¼ yard (.23 m) of light fabric for half-square triangles

¾ yard (.7 m) of backing fabric

1 piece of batting, 30 inches square (76.2 cm)

⅕ yard (.2 m) of binding fabric

tools

Basic Patchwork Kit (page 8)

Quilting tape (for sandwiching the quilt)

Walking foot (optional)

finished size

22½ inches square (57.2 cm)

seam allowance

¼ inch (6 mm) unless otherwise noted

get started

1 Each Jacob's Ladder block is made from two 4-patch units and two half-square triangles, assembled as shown **(A)**. Decide what two colors (1 dark, 1 light) you want to use for the four-patch and what two colors (1 dark, 1 light) to use for the half-square triangles.

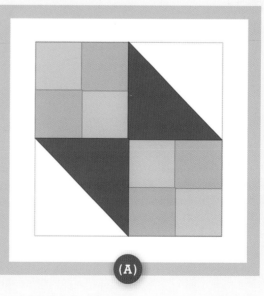

(A)

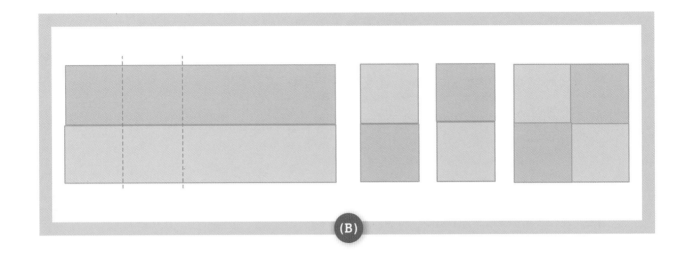

(B)

2 Make 60 four-patch units as follows:

- Cut five strips each from the dark and light fabrics (10 total) that measure 1½ inches (3.8 cm) x the width of the fabric (from selvedge to selvedge).

- Stitch each light strip of fabric to a dark strip of fabric to make five sets of strips. Press the seam allowances toward the darker strips.

- Cut across the strips to make 1½ inch (3.8 cm) segments. Cut 25 units from each strip; you need a total of 120 units **(B)**. Square up the leading edge when necessary; you will have several extra inches to play with as you cut segments. Sew pairs of segments into four-patch units, pressing seams in a consistent manner. Each four-patch unit will measure 2½ inches square (6.4 cm).

3 Make 61 half-square triangles as follows:

- Cut 31 squares from both light and dark fabrics (62 squares total), each measuring 2⁷/₈ inches square (7.3 cm).

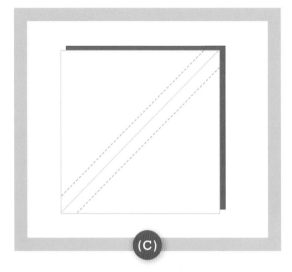

(C)

- On the wrong side of the light-colored fabric, use a pencil to draw a diagonal line from corner to corner. With right sides facing, match up each light-colored square with a dark-colored square. Stitch a scant ¼ inch (6 mm) seam on both sides of the marked line (**C**). Cut along the drawn line.

- Open up the block and press the seam toward the dark fabric. Each half-square triangle will measure 2½ inches square (6.4 cm).

> *Tip If you prefer, cut the squares larger—say, 3³/4 inches square (9.5 cm)—and then trim them down to the correct size. It adds an extra step but can be well worth it, particularly when working with such small units.*

4 The Jacob's Ladder quilt top consists of 11 rows of 11 blocks. Refer to the sample for the correct layout and orientation of each of the 121 units.

- Carefully arrange the blocks as pictured. Stitch the blocks together in rows, beginning with the top row (which starts and ends with a half-square triangle unit).

- When all 11 rows are stitched, press the seams in the first row to the right, the seams in the second row to the left. Continue pressing the seams, alternating the direction for each consecutive row. This way matching seams will lock together when rows are sewn together.

- Stitch the rows together, matching up seams. When the quilt top is complete, press seams open.

5 Cut the backing fabric and the batting several inches larger than the quilt top on all sides. Make a quilt sandwich of the backing, batting, and quilt top, then pin or baste all layers in place. Quilt as desired.

6 Use a rotary cutter to square up your edges. Make bias strips from the binding fabric and bind the quilt (page 17).

I spy

Introducing the "Swiss Army knife" of doll quilts: this project morphs from doll quilt into pillow into cozy sleeping bag.

handmade by **HEATHER BOSTIC**

fabric & such

24 English paper piecing hexagons, 1½ inch (3.8 cm) wide (or use the hexagon template)

24 pieces of scrap fabric for fussy cut hexagons

1 piece of cotton or linen fabric for front (fabric A), 19 inches square (48.3 cm)

1 piece of solid cotton or muslin fabric for lining (fabric B), 19 inches square (48.3 cm)

1 piece of batting, 19 inches square (48.3 cm)

Embroidery floss in two coordinating colors

½ yard (.5 m) of complementary print for pocket/pillow backing (fabric C) (optional)

tools

Basic Patchwork Kit (page 8)

Template (page 122), if using

Office paper for paper piecing

Pinking shears

finished size

16 x 16¾ inches (40.6 x 42.5 cm)

seam allowance

½ inch (1.3 mm), unless otherwise noted

get started

1 Create the hexagons as follows:

- Using the English paper piecing templates (or 24 hexagon templates from page 122), pin the 24 scrap fabrics to the paper hexagons as desired to showcase a specific motif (page 10), and cut them out, adding a ½-inch (1.3 cm) seam allowance.

- Fold the seam allowance to the back and baste each hexagon.

- Press and arrange the hexagons into your preferred design.

- Use a ladder stitch to hand sew the hexagons together.

- Press the design, then remove the basting stitches and paper. Press again.

2 Make a quilt sandwich of the lining fabric (B), batting, front fabric A, and hexagon design, then pin all layers in place. Using a sewing machine, topstitch around the inside edge of the hexagon design.

3 Using two coordinating colors of embroidery floss, hand quilt two decorative rows of stitches outside the perimeter to outline the design. Or, if you'd like to make the pocket/pillow backing, set the quilt sandwich aside and continue with the next step.

4 Cut backing fabric C into two rectangles at the following sizes:

- 18 x 26 inches (45.7 x 66 cm)
- 18 x 16 inches (45.7 x 40.6 cm)

5 Fold each rectangle in half lengthwise, wrong sides facing, and press to the following sizes:

- 18 x 13 inches (45.7 x 33 cm)
- 18 x 8 inches (45.7 x 20.3 cm)

6 Topstitch ¼ inch (6 mm) from the folded edges on both rectangles.

7 Lay the quilt top on a flat surface, right side up. With right sides facing, pin the smaller rectangle to the top, aligning raw edges on three sides. Pin the larger rectangle on the opposite end, aligning raw edges and overlapping the folded edges of the two rectangles. Stitch a ¼-inch (6 mm) seam around the border of the quilt while backstitching over the backing's opening. Clip the corners and trim the seam allowance with pinking shears. Turn right side out and press.

slumber party!

This clever quilty transforms in many ways, from doll quilt to pillow cover to super cute sleeping bag for a dolly— or bunnies—on the go.

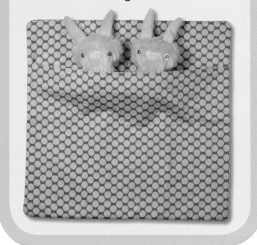

patches and lace

Hand-tie this homespun lovely, and dress it up with a few vintage doilies from your own collection. If you're handy with a hook, we've included a pattern for a simple crocheted doily, too.

handmade by MARGIE OOMEN

fabric & such

¹⁄₈ yard (.15 m) each of eight complementary solid-colored fabrics

½ yard (.5 m) of gray madras cotton fabric

1 piece of batting, 12 x 10 inches (30.5 x 25.4 cm)

12 to 15 small crocheted lace medallions (or make your own!)

Embroidery thread in contrasting colors

tools

Basic Patchwork Kit (page 8)

finished size

12 x 10 inches (30.5 x 25.4 cm)

seam allowance

¼ inch (6 mm) unless otherwise noted

1 Measure and cut out twenty 3-inch (7.6 cm) squares from the complementary fabrics. Cut three each of four colors and two each of the remaining four colors.

2 Cut 12 x 10-inch (30.5 x 25.4 cm) rectangles from both the gray madras and the batting, and set them aside.

3 Lay out your square blocks so that no two adjoining squares are the same color. Stitch the blocks together in rows, and then stitch the rows together. Press flat.

4 Hand sew lace medallions to random squares in a pleasing pattern.

5 Make a quilt sandwich of the remaining gray madras, batting, and quilt top, then pin or baste all layers in place.

6 Thread an embroidery needle with a length of embroidery floss in a complementary color. Tie the quilt together by stitching through all three layers at each of the 12 block intersections (the corners of each square), tying off the thread at each intersection on the top layer.

7 Make ¼-inch (6 mm) bias tape from the gray madras fabric, or use premade tape in a complementary color, and bind the quilt (page 17). For a special touch, hand sew the edge of the binding with the embroidery thread, using a cross stitch pattern along the border. Press the finished doll quilt.

crochet your own medallions

If you can't find the perfect vintage doilies or medallions to use on your quilt, stitch them up yourself! First, grab these: size 12 cotton crochet thread, size 6 crochet hook, and one large-eye yarn needle. Then:

1 Chain five stitches and join to form a circle.

2 Chain two, then work 10 double crochet stitches inside the circle. Join the round.

3 Chain two, then work two double crochet stitches in each space. Join the round.

4 Chain two, then work three double crochet stitches in each space. Join the round.

5 Cut the thread, fasten off, and use a large-eye needle to weave in loose ends.

dancing rabbit

There is so much hand-embroidered goodness here that you'll be doing a little dance of your own.

handmade by ANDREA ZUILL

fabric & such

¼ yard (.23 m) of fabric for the four corners (fabric A)

¼ yard (.23 m) of neutral fabric for the top and side rectangles (fabric B)

¼ yard (.23 m) of print fabric for the center background (fabric C)

¼ yard (.23 m) of white fabric for the rabbit appliqué (fabric D)

Dark thread for basting

1 scrap of fabric for the rabbit's eyes

2 fat quarters of complementary cotton fabrics for the corner flowers

¼ yard (.23 m) of cotton backing fabric

1 piece of cotton batting, 30 x 20 inches (76.2 x 50.8 cm)

Neutral hand quilting thread

Embroidery floss in various colors

tools

Basic Patchwork Kit (page 8)

Templates (page 122)

finished size

22¼ x 17 inches (56.5 x 42.3 cm)

seam allowance

¼ inch (6 mm)

get started

1 Cut out the following fabric pieces (A):

- From fabric A: four 6-inch (15.2 cm) squares for the corners

- From fabric B: two 10½ x 6-inch (26.7 x 15.2 cm) rectangles for the top and bottom, and two 6 x 16½-inch (15.2 x 41.9 cm) rectangles for the sides

- From fabric C: one 10 x 16½-inch (25.4 x 41.9 cm) rectangle

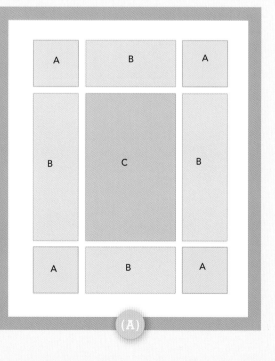

(A)

2 Stitch the quilt top together as follows:

- Stitch the fabric A squares to the top and bottom of the fabric B side rectangles. Press the seams.

- Stitch the fabric B top and bottom pieces to the fabric C center piece. Press the seams.

- Stitch the side panels to the center panel. Press the seams.

3 Enlarge the rabbit template and cut it out. Place the template onto solid white cotton and trace the image 1/8 inch (3 mm) larger than the template. Cut out the rabbit. Attach it to the center of the quilt, as follows:

- Center the rabbit shape and pin it into place. With dark thread, baste 1/8 inch (3 mm) from the fabric edge.

- Thread a needle with the hand quilting thread and knot the end. Unthread about 1/2 inch (1.3 cm) of basting on the rabbit. Use the needle to turn under the edge of the rabbit about 1/8 inch (3 mm).

- Use the blind stitch to sew the rabbit to the quilt top, removing a little of the basting at a time as you work your way around the edges.

- Use the template to cut out the rabbit's eyes from scrap fabric and appliqué in place.

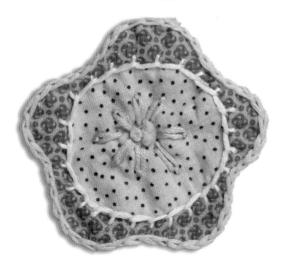

4 Enlarge the flower templates for petals and centers. Cut four flowers and four centers 1/8 inch (3 mm) larger than the template. With a fabric pencil or straight pins, mark the 2-inch (5.1 cm) margin for binding on all sides of the quilt top. In the space that's left, center each flower in a corner square, with the flower center on top. Use the same technique as with the rabbit to appliqué the flowers and centers.

5 Embroider the rabbit and flowers as you like. To copy the design shown, use six strands of embroidery floss and stitch as follows:

the rabbit

- Stem stitch in light blue floss around the white rabbit.

- Use oversized seed stitch in light blue floss for the fur texture.

- Use black floss around the rabbit's eyes and to create nose and mouth.

- Satin stitch white eye highlights.

center panel

- Maidenhair stitch right along the seam in orange floss.

- Create french knots along both sides of the seam, at the top of the maidenhair stitch strands, in dark teal.

corner flowers

- Chain stitch with bright yellow floss around the flower outline.

- Running stitch outside of the flower in burgundy.

- Blanket stitch around the flower center in white floss.

- Use a series of single chain stitches to create a flower within the flower center in medium blue floss.

- Stitch three bright-yellow French knots in the centers of the embroidered flowers.

corner square embroidery

- Create a row of fly stitches, leaving a little space between each stitch, on the two inner edges of each corner square, using yellow floss.

- Chain stitch between each fly stitch using medium blue floss.

6 To join the quilt top, batting, and backing:

- Cut the backing fabric 2 inches (5.1 cm) smaller than your quilt top on each side.

- Cut the batting the same size as the quilt back.

- Make a quilt sandwich of the backing, batting, and quilt top, taping the backing to the work surface. The quilt top will be 2 inches (5.1 cm) larger on all sides.

- Starting in the center and working outward, pin baste the layers together.

- Now baste your quilt sandwich together with large stitches, in a color that contrasts well with your fabric.

7 Quilt as desired.

8 To bind the quilt, fold one edge of the quilt top to the back, making a 1-inch (2.5 cm) double-fold hem. Pin in place, and use a blind stitch to hand sew the folded edge. Repeat to bind the remaining edges.

red riding hood

A pretty Dresden plate, fabulous themed fabrics, and a sweet stitched Little Red, this quilty is ready for storytime.

handmade by **KERRI HORSLEY**

fabric & such

½ yard (.5 m) of white fabric for background

Scraps of assorted fabric

½ yard (.5 m) of backing fabric

1 piece of batting, 20 inches square (50.8 cm)

½ yard (.5 m) of coordinating binding fabric

tools

Basic Patchwork Kit (page 8)

Templates (page 123)

Dresden plate ruler (optional)

finished size

20 inches (50.8 cm) square

seam allowance

¼ inch (6 mm)

get started

1 Cut a 10-inch (25.4 cm) square of white fabric. Enlarge the embroidery template and transfer the pattern to the center of the square. Using an embroidery hoop and floss in colors of your choice, embroider the pattern using a backstitch. For the dots on the cape and mushrooms, stitch French knots (page 13). Once the embroidery is finished, set aside.

2 To make the Dresden plate block:

- Choose 20 coordinating scrap fabrics that will complement the colors in your embroidery.

- Cut each piece to measure 3½ x 5 inches (8.9 x 12.7 cm).

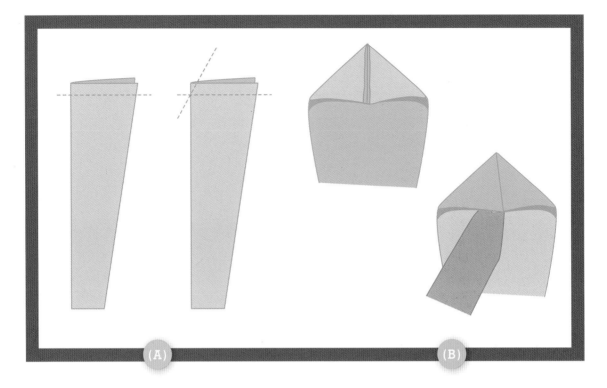

(A)   (B)

- Place each fabric piece under the Dresden plate ruler between the 1-inch (2.5 cm) line and the 6-inch (15.2 cm) line, and use the lines as a guide to cut each of your scraps into "petals." Or enlarge and use the template to cut each petal shape. Cut out 20 petals. Leave the wide ends straight across for now. Press each petal.

- Fold each petal in half vertically with right sides together. Stitch a ¼ inch (6 mm) seam along the top edge of the fabric, and then trim the corner (A).

- Finger press the seam open, and then turn the petal right side out. Use a turning tool to push the point fully out (B). Press each petal and make sure your stitching is aligned straight.

- Arrange your petals in a circle in the order you prefer them. To assemble the circle, stitch five petals together along the sides, one at a time, right sides together. Repeat three more times until you have four sets of five stitched petals.

- Stitch two of the sets together, then stitch together the other two sets. Press seams open, then stitch these two halves of the pattern together to make the whole circle. Press seams again.

3 From the remaining white fabric, cut an 18-inch (45.7 cm) square. Fold it into quarters and press. Center the stitched Dresden plate on top, aligning the points of the top, bottom, and side petals with the folded lines. Pin each petal to the background so it lays flat, then topstitch the Dresden plate around the inner circle and the points, stitching as close to the edges as you can.

4 To attach the embroidery to the center:

- On the back of the embroidered fabric, trace a circle that measures ½ inch (1.3 cm) larger on all sides than the inner circle of the Dresden plate.

- Cut another piece of white fabric the same size as the embroidered square. In the center of the white piece, cut a 2-inch (5.1 cm) slit so you are able to turn the piece right side out later.

- Pin the embroidered square and the white fabric right sides together, and then stitch along the circle you traced.

- Turn the circle right side out through the slit and use the pointer stick to push out the fabric edges evenly into a circle. Press.

5 Center the embroidery circle on top of the Dresden plate and pin in place. Topstitch the outer edge of the circle to the background.

6 Make a quilt sandwich of the backing, batting, and quilt top, then pin or baste all layers in place. Quilt as desired.

7 Cut strips from the binding fabric and bind the quilt (page 17).

scrappy asterisks

Bring together opposites with appliqué, patchwork, straight stitch quilting, and hand stitches. Your favorite dolly or softie will thank you for the matching apron, too.

handmade by **AMANDA CARESTIO**

fabric & such

9 pieces of fabric in 3 shades of solid gray, each about 4- to 5-inches (10.2 to 12.7 cm) square

Scraps of tan linen and gray print fabrics

7 scraps of yellow fabrics, each about 6 inches (25.4 cm) square

2 fat quarters (45.7 x 55.9 cm) of yellow fabric for asterisk appliqué and binding

Paper-backed fusible web, ¾ yard (.3 m)

1 fat quarter (45.7 x 55.9 cm) of backing fabric

1 piece of batting, 18 inches square (45.7 cm)

Cream embroidery floss

Cream and yellow sewing thread

tools

Basic Patchwork Kit (page 8)

Template (page 122)

finished size

15¾ inches square (40 cm)

seam allowance

¼ inch (6 mm)

get started

1 Cut nine 4- to 5-inch squares (10.2 to 12.7 cm) from the solid gray fabrics.

2 From the tan and gray print fabrics, cut strips that measure 1½ to 3 inches (3.8 to 7.6 cm) wide and about 5 to 8 inches (12.7 to 20.3 cm) long. Randomly piece small rectangles of yellow fabric into these strips, varying the width and length of the rectangles. You'll need 18 strips total, two for each solid gray square.

3 Stitch the strips to the left and bottom edges of each gray square, alternating the placement of the yellow rectangles (A).

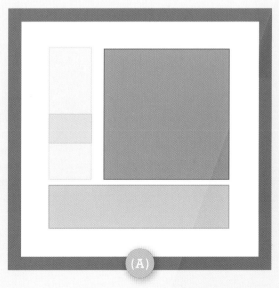

(A)

4 Iron each square and press the seams out. Cut each square to 5½ inches (14 cm), using a ruler square. While you're cutting, vary the width of the strips and the size of the gray squares.

Tip For a wonkier look, rotate the ruler squares so the gray squares are pitched at different angles.

5 Cut nine 4½-inch squares (11.4 cm) of yellow fabric, using the scraps and fat quarters, then cut and fuse squares of fusible web onto the back of each of your fabric squares. Enlarge and cut out the asterisk template, and use it to trace the asterisk shape onto the back of each square of webbing. Cut out the asterisk shapes, introducing some variations to the sizes and angles as you cut.

6 Fuse an asterisk in the center of each gray square, making sure you leave room around the top and right edges for the seam allowance. Zigzag stitch around the perimeter of each asterisk shape with yellow or cream thread, using a medium-width zigzag and a fairly short stitch length.

Tip The centers of the asterisks will likely pucker as you stitch around them. Don't worry: you'll stitch the centers flat in a later step.

7 Stitch the squares together into three rows and then stitch the rows together. Square up the quilt top if needed.

8 Make a quilt sandwich of the backing, batting, and quilt top, and then pin or baste all layers in place.

9 Stitch around the inside edge of each appliqué shape just inside the zigzag stitch lines. Stitch just outside the edge of several of the shapes. Create several lines of stitching through the left and bottom strips of each block, leaving some spaces open for hand stitches later (B).

scrappy apron!

When it comes to dolls and doll quilts, it's hard to resist accessorizing just a little bit. And how about a cute matching apron? With leftover scraps from the quilt and a length of twill tape, follow these simple steps:

1 Cut a 5-inch (12.7 cm) square from the main gray fabric and a 5 x 2-inch (12.7 x 5.1 cm) strip from one of the prints. Stitch the strip to the bottom of the gray square. Fold under the left, bottom, and side edges by ¼ inch (6 mm), and stitch them in place. Fold over the top edge 1 inch (2.5 cm), and stitch it in place to make a casing for the apron strap.

2 Shrink the template from your quilt, and use it to cut a fusible-backed appliqué shape from yellow fabric...or just wing it! Fuse and then stitch the appliqué shape in place on the apron front.

3 Cut a 1-inch (2.5 cm) square and stitch the left, bottom, and right edges to the apron front to create a teeny pocket.

4 Feed a length of twill tape through the casing at the top of the apron.

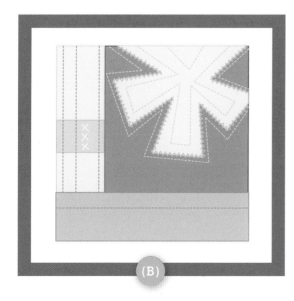

(B)

10 Square up and trim off the excess batting and backing fabric.

11 Cut and piece together a 3-inch-wide (7.6 cm) binding strip using the yellow fat quarters and other fabric scraps. Bind the quilt (page 17).

12 Using the cream embroidery floss, hand sew lines of running stitches and cross-stitches across the quilt—the wonkier, the better.

spiderweb redux

A new take on an old favorite—and the perfect way to use up your most favorite bits of fabric—this quilt incorporates the traditional spiderweb pattern, only in reverse.

handmade by **CATHY GAUBERT**

fabric & such

Scraps of 16 fabrics, at least ½ to 2 x 5 inches (1.3 to 5.1 cm x 12.7 cm)

½ yard (.5 m) of fabric for background

½ yard (.5 m) of backing fabric

1 piece of batting, 23 inches square (58.4 cm)

3 yards (2.75 m) of binding, 3 inches (7.6 cm) wide

Embroidery floss in a complementary color

tools

Basic Patchwork Kit (page 8)

Templates (page 121)

Paper for foundation piecing

Spray bottle (optional)

finished size

22 inches square (55.9 cm)

seam allowance

¼ inch (6 mm) unless otherwise noted

get started

1 The quilt top is pieced together from four segments or blocks. The instructions are for making one block, so you will repeat steps 2 through 7 to make all four blocks. Start by enlarging, tracing, and cutting four copies of template 1 from the office paper, labeling the corners A, B, and C as indicated. The A corner will be the center point of the block.

2 Now for the foundation piecing (page 11). No need to overthink this step; just grab your scrap fabrics and sew!

> *Tip Don't forget to shorten your stitch length while foundation piecing on paper; this will make the removal of the template much easier.*

- Place a fabric strip right side up over tip (A) of the paper template and stitch (A).

- Place a second strip, wrong side up, on top of the first stitched strip allowing about an 1/8 inch (3 mm) of the top of the first strip to show (B). Stitch.

- Press the second strip up so that the right side is facing you. Place a third strip on top of the second one, wrong side up. Stitch and press up. Continue in this manner until the paper template is covered, pressing as you go (C).

3 Turn the now-covered template over. Use a ruler and rotary cutter to trim the fabric edges flush with the template edges. With a spray bottle, spritz the paper template and carefully tear away the template along the stitch lines. Remove any stray paper bits, and press your patchwork piece.

4 Repeat steps 2 and 3 to fill the remaining templates, for a total of four patchwork pieces.

5 From selvedge to selvedge, cut a strip of background fabric 6 inches (15.2 cm) wide. Enlarge and cut out template 2, then use a pencil to trace the template onto the fabric eight times. Label the corners of the triangles.

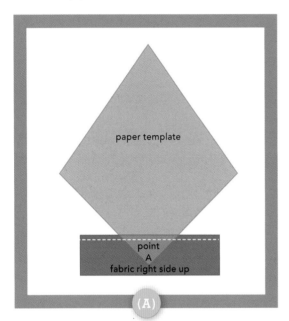

(A)

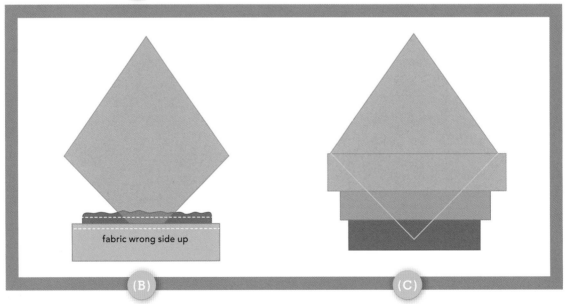

(B)   (C)

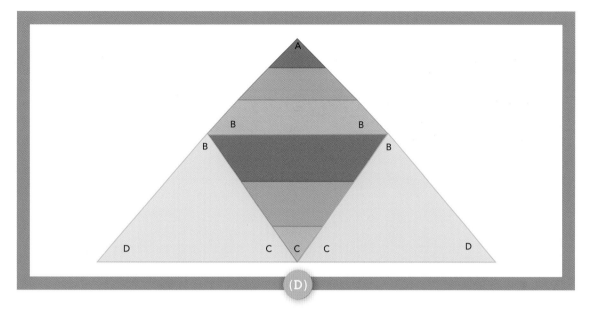

(D)

6 Lay out two background triangles and one pieced diamond (D), matching up the corners as labeled. With right sides facing, stitch from B to C on both sides of the pieced diamond. Repeat this step with the remaining diamonds and triangles.

7 You now have four large triangles and are ready to complete the first block of the quilt top:

- Match up two of the pieced triangles, with right sides together. Stitch the pieces together from A to D, taking care to match the seams at point B. Press the seam open.

- Repeat for the remaining two pieced triangles. Press the seam open.

- Now, stitch these two pieces together, taking care to match seams. Press. Square up the block to measure 11½ inches square (29.2 cm).

8 You have now made the first block. Repeat steps 2 through 7 to make three more blocks.

9 Taking care to match your seams, pin and then stitch the four blocks together.

10 Make a quilt sandwich of the backing, batting, and quilt top, then pin or baste all layers in place. Quilt by machine or by hand as desired.

11 Using the remaining scrap fabrics, trim pieces 3 inches (7.6 cm) wide and in varying lengths. Sew pieces end to end to create approximately 3 yards of patchwork binding. Bind the quilt (page 17).

templates

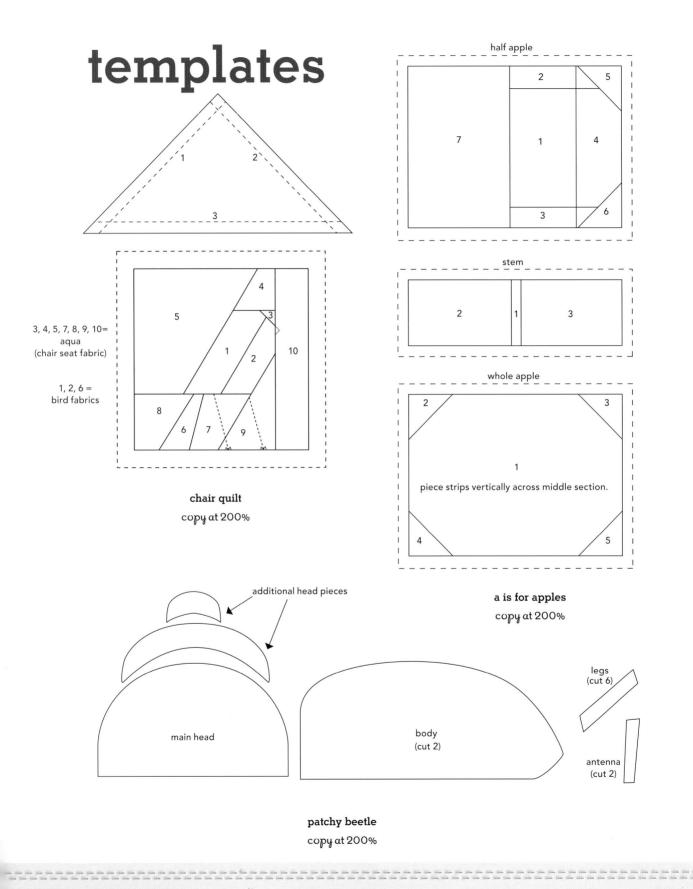

half apple

	2		5
7	1	4	
	3		6

3, 4, 5, 7, 8, 9, 10=
aqua
(chair seat fabric)

1, 2, 6 =
bird fabrics

chair quilt
copy at 200%

stem

| 2 | 1 | 3 |

whole apple

2		3
	1	
piece strips vertically across middle section.		
4		5

a is for apples
copy at 200%

additional head pieces

main head

body
(cut 2)

legs
(cut 6)

antenna
(cut 2)

patchy beetle
copy at 200%

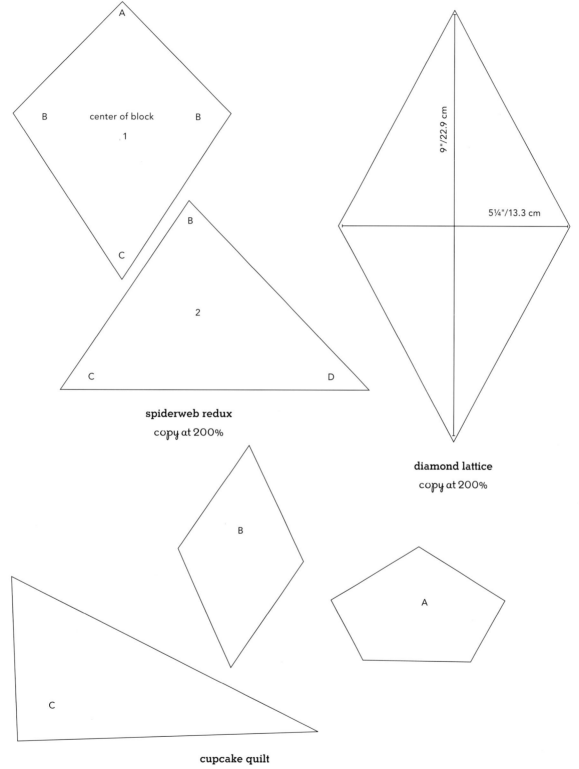

A

B   center of block   B

.1

B

C

2

C   D

spiderweb redux

copy at 200%

9"/22.9 cm

5¼"/13.3 cm

diamond lattice

copy at 200%

B

A

C

cupcake quilt

copy at 200%

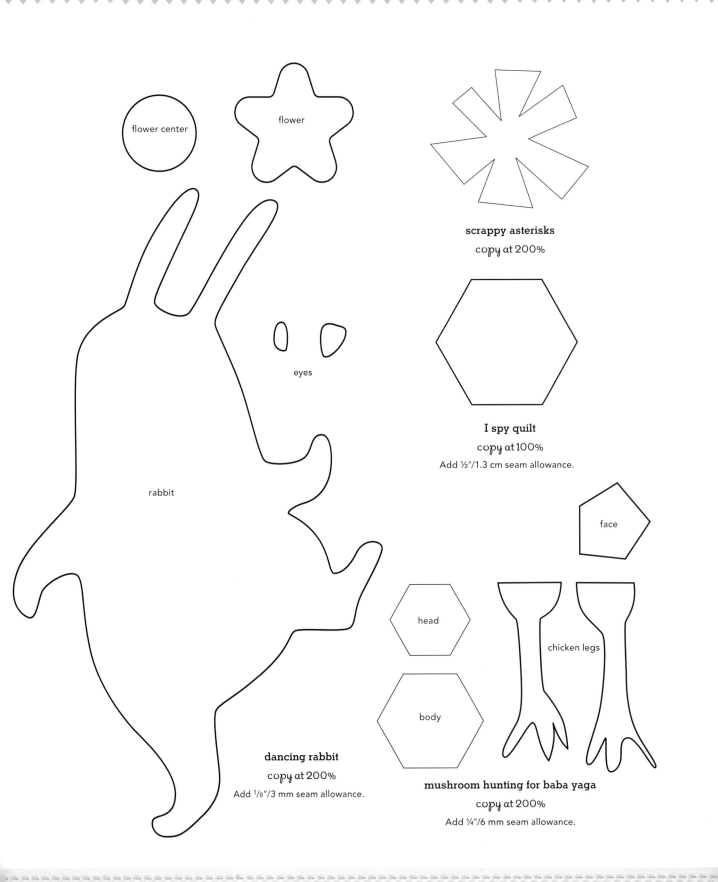

flower center

flower

scrappy asterisks
copy at 200%

eyes

I spy quilt
copy at 100%
Add ½"/1.3 cm seam allowance.

face

rabbit

head

chicken legs

body

dancing rabbit
copy at 200%
Add ⅛"/3 mm seam allowance.

mushroom hunting for baba yaga
copy at 200%
Add ¼"/6 mm seam allowance.

red riding hood
copy at 100%

Dresden petal template

mod log cabin
copy at 100%

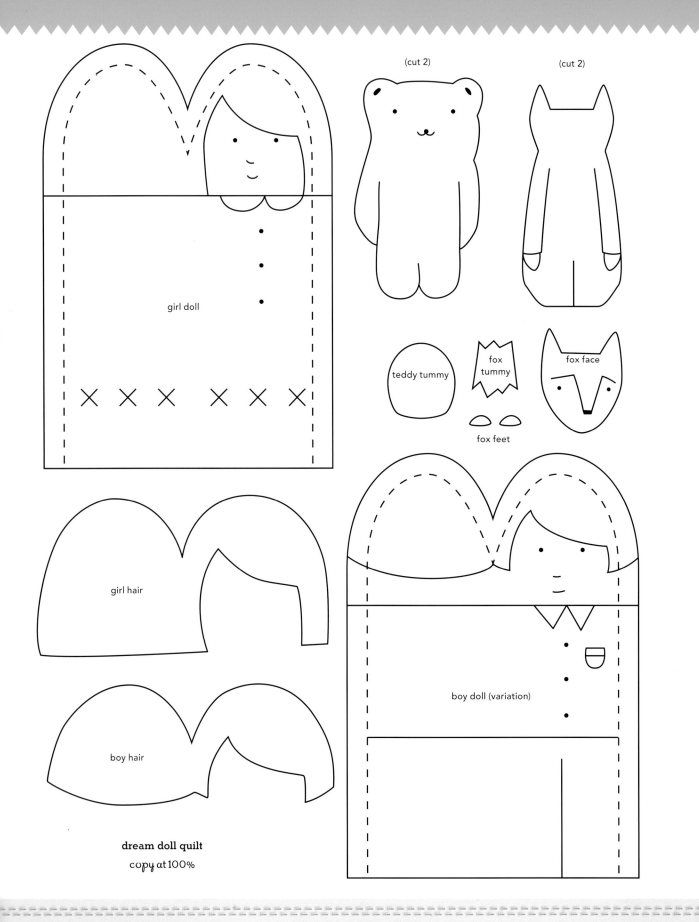

(cut 2)

(cut 2)

girl doll

teddy tummy

fox tummy

fox face

fox feet

girl hair

boy hair

boy doll (variation)

dream doll quilt
copy at 100%

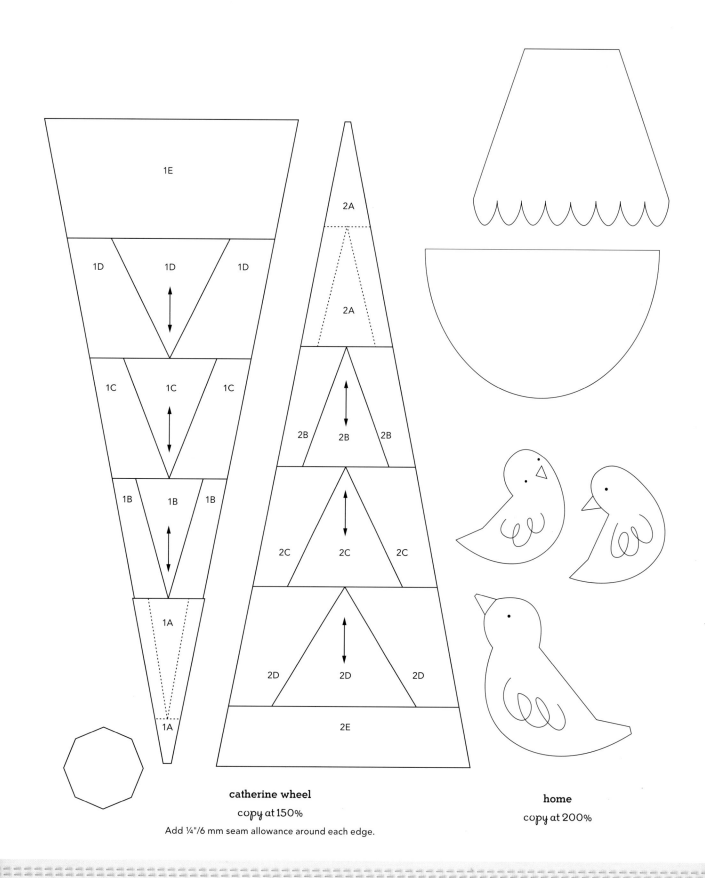

catherine wheel

copy at 150%

Add ¼"/6 mm seam allowance around each edge.

home

copy at 200%

about the designers

John Q. Adams is a husband and father of three who enjoys sewing and quilting in his spare time. Inspired by the growing number of crafting blogs and the emergence of vibrant, modern quilting fabrics in the textile industry, John convinced his wife to teach him how to use her sewing machine in 2004 and hasn't looked back. He started his popular blog, QuiltDad.com, in 2008 to share his love of patchwork with others. Since then, John has become very active in online quilting communities. Today, he applies his modern quilting aesthetic by designing quilt patterns for both fabric designers and companies and contributing frequently to creative blogs, books, and other collaborative endeavors. John is also a co-founder of the popular e-magazine *Fat Quarterly*. John and his family live in Cary, North Carolina.

Jessica Bennett has been making quilts since she was a teenager and still uses her grandfather's Singer to do her machine quilting. In a tiny house near downtown Salt Lake City, she does her sewing with a husband, two little boys, and a kitty underfoot. Her favorite quilt designs are simple and modern, yet crooked and unexpected. Photography is another love of hers, so visit her website for lots of photos of her unique quilts: www.urban-patchwork.com.

Katherine "SueSue" Bollinger has been a creator of "stuff" most of her life. Her fondest memories from childhood are filled with making holiday decorations and sewing and creating with her mom and siblings (all ten of them!). Through her life, she has sewn clothing and toys for herself, her four children (and now her grandchildren), family, and friends. Her love of all things handmade is visible throughout her 100-year-old family home, and she believes that scraps of anything can be turned into art! Visit her at http://lagniappe-suesueb.blogspot.com.

Heather Bostic lives in beautiful Portland, Oregon. She's an adoring wife, the mother of two beautiful boys, and an autism activist. Sewing was an easy choice for relaxation while raising a child with autism, although what started out as a hobby has turned into a manic compulsion that has an appetite of its very own. She just can't help herself! Combine that with her Flickr and blog life, and you have one serious non-stop party! This is her—keeping it real—in all her glory: http://alamodefabric.blogspot.com.

Amanda Carestio, an editor at Lark, keeps herself busy with various stitching projects, linoleum block prints, and costume-oriented crafting pursuits. When she's not hunkered over a craft book, working feverishly at her mother's old Singer, exploring the Blue Ridge Mountains, surfing Flickr, or plotting her next trip to the fabric store, Amanda enjoys spending quiet time with her hubby and her brindle squad in Asheville, North Carolina. Amanda is the author of *Fa La La La Felt* and *Stash Happy Felt*, both published by Lark, and she blogs at www.digsandbean.blogspot.com.

Malka Dubrawsky worked for several years primarily as a fiber artist and was lucky enough to be included in some prestigious shows and publications such as Quilt National, Visions, and *Fiberarts: Design Book 7*. More recently she's been busy making functional textiles, though still primarily out of her own hand-dyed and patterned fabric. To this end, she has turned her attention to crafting quilts, pillows, and other sundries for sale in her online store: http://stitchindye.etsy.com. Malka writes and designs patterns and has been published in magazines such as *Quilting Arts*, *Stitch*, and several books including *Sweater Surgery*, *Quilts, Baby!*, *Pretty Little Mini Quilts*, *Whip Up Mini Quilts*, and *Quilting Art*. Her first book, *Color Your Cloth: A Quilter's Guide to Dyeing and Patterning Fabric*, was published by Lark and a second book, *Fresh Quilting: Fearless, Color, Design, and Inspiration* was released by Interweave Press. Read more about Malka and her work at http://stitchindye.blogspot.com.

Brioni Greenberg has been sewing on and off for most of her life—which was inevitable, as she's the daughter of a tailor and dressmaker. It's in her genes. As a child she made handbags and doll clothes and was never very satisfied with how they turned out. She received her first "grown-up" sewing machine when she was 21—studying textile design and technology—and had marvelous fun sewing bits of knitting, paper, masking tape, lumpy handmade felt, and anything else that would fit under the foot. She made her first quilt about four or five years ago, never imagining that it would suck her in and lead to the biggest obsession she's ever had! She works full time, so her time is limited, but she does manage to squeeze quilting into just about every waking moment and collects fabric like others collect Lladro figurines! She blogs at www.flossyblossy.blogspot.com.

Rita Hodge is the proud mother of a daughter and son. Together with her husband, they live in Melbourne, Australia. Making quilts is how she spends every spare moment. She started her blog in April 2009 to journal her quilting adventures and has been overwhelmed with the positive response to her work and blog. She has also, at the request of her readers, started writing quilt patterns. Her aim is to inspire everyone to sew or be creative a little every day. Visit her at www.redpepperquilts.com.

Aneela Hoey graduated from Winchester School of Art with a BA in printed textile design in 1994 and is now a fabric designer for Moda Fabrics. She can always be found surrounded by fabric and stitching something or other. She lives in Berkshire, England, with her husband and two young daughters. A keen embroiderer and quilter, she also writes her own patterns and tutorials, which can be found at her blog: http://comfortstitching.typepad.co.uk.

Kerri Horsley is a mother to six sweet children, wife to a loving husband, crafter, and blogger who lives in the Seattle, Washington, area. She is a former Montessori teacher who tries to incorporate its teachings into her home. Kerri was born in Tehran, Iran, and spent a couple years in Shanghai, China—maybe that's why she loves to travel. Her spring and summer days are often spent taking trips to the beach and parks with her family. Kerri also runs a small business, Sew Deerly Loved, with the help of her devoted husband. You can find her work at www.sewdeerlyloved.etsy.com and www.sewdeerly-loved.com. Make sure to stop by her blog and say hi: www.lovelylittlehandmades.blogspot.com.

Lucinda Jones began sewing at the age of six, making doll clothes with fabric scraps left over from projects by her extremely talented seamstress of a mother. Quilting has been her passion for the past decade. Not one to follow a pattern, she is self-taught and an admirer of Gwen Marston and *Liberated Quilting*. Lucinda likes her self-designed, playful quilts to tell stories and have a sense of humor. Her work draws upon her love of antiques, horticulture, and nature. She quilts daily in a restored 1819 farmhouse in upstate New York. She can be found online at www.septemberbird.wordpress.com.

Rebeka Lambert lives with her husband and three children on the outskirts of Baton Rouge, Louisiana. She inherited her love of sewing from her mother and grand-mother. She enjoys creating bags, purses, quilts, and her own sewing pattern line. Although she put crafting on hold during her first years as a mother, Beki is back at it thanks in part to the discovery of craft blogs. The daily feedback and sharing of ideas through blogging keeps her inspired. Beki has contributed to Lark's Pretty Little series, *Craft Hope*, and Interweave's *Stitch* magazine. Visit her online at www.artsycraftybabe.typepad.com and www.artsycraftybabe.etsy.com.

Penny Layman remembers her mom sewing clothing for her and her siblings. In fact, one of her favorite photos shows her with her mom, sister, and cousin in matching seafoam green polyester dresses. She has been sewing on and off since she was six or seven, mixing in a few other things she really enjoys—like crochet, papermaking, backpacking, and kayaking. She blogs at www.sewtakeahike.typepad.com and would love to hear from you!

Amy Proff Lyons is an artist, a wife to one incredibly patient man, and a mother to three whiz-bang kids. She never met a medium she didn't like. Don't ask her to choose a favorite. Seriously, it would be like asking her to choose a favorite child. Okay, if she had to choose: jewelry design (including metalsmithing, enameling, lampwork-ing); designing cute stationery (digital illustrations, hand drawn one-offs, collage); and sewing (and quilting). To find more of Amy's work visit her at www.aplcreations.com.

Margie Oomen is married to the wonderful father of their four talented children, a rural physician, a nature lover, a collector, and a maker of things as far back as she can remember. When she isn't healing the sick or exploring the forests, you might find her creating magic in her studio. She is self-taught in craft, and her skills include crochet, knitting, felting, hand stitching, hand dyeing, patchwork, screen printing, and, most recently, weaving. She lives with her fabulous family, three vintage hankie-adorned cats, and a snail named Fern in a century-old home in Ontario, Canada. If you want to learn more, go to www.resurrectionfern.ca and click away.

Jen Osborn is a mixed media artist, writer, and art quil-ter from Michigan. She loves nothing more than giving you a peek into her enormous imagination by stitching it all up into art that encourages you to not only look, but also touch. Her first book, *Mixed and Stitched*, was released in June 2011. You can find her in the pages of *Cloth Paper Scissors*, and numerous Somerset publications. She also teaches at CrescenDOH's Creative Lab. You can get a better peek inside her noggin through on her blogs: We're All Mad Here! (http://blog.themessynest.com) and 365 days of 40 (http://365daysof40.themessynest.com).

Susan Sobon is the wife of George and the mom of Chloe. They have all lived in Gurnee, Illinois, for the past 5 years, but Susan has been a Midwestern girl her whole life (it's where she acquired her love for quilting and making softies). Working in a quilt shop part-time adds to her interest in fiber—so does her passion for collecting Japanese craft books. On her free days, if she's not quilting, you might find her at a flea market looking for all things vintage, or baking up something yummy in her kitchen. Susan finds inspiration all over, but especially on Flickr and in her craft books. Visit her online by searching for "chickenfoot" on Flickr or going to her blog: http://www.iamchickenfoot.blogspot.com.

Amanda Woodward-Jennings is the wife of an amazing Porkchop, lover of scissors and thread, list maker, photograph taker, cat blog reader, and candy cane obsessive. She owns a small pattern company and loves handwork of all varieties. When she's not sewing, she's canning, baking, and throwing dance parties.

Andrea Zuill has always created art. She started by painting bizarre and whimsical characters in oil paints and watercolor, and while she still paints she also feels the need for a more tactile form of art. For years she collected fabric, yet it all went unused. When helping a friend with their art quilt, Andrea was able to embroider and hand quilt for the first time. Much to her surprise, she found she liked to hand sew. Thus began her journey of combining old-fashioned techniques with contemporary folk images. You can read her articles, view her work, and download embroidery patterns from her blog: http://zuill.us/andreablog.

about the author

Cathy Gaubert is a wife, a momma, and a maker of things. Her days are filled with the antics of three sweet girlies, and the kitchen table is filled with more works-in-progress than you can shake a stick at. Her favorites include linen, wool felt, gingham, all sorts of patchwork-y goodness, children's drawings, handstitching, fairy tales, forests, family, Clotilda Plantation, Neil Gaiman, Neko Case, Ben Labat and the Happy Devil, narwhals, kisses that have dance parties on her children's cheeks, Flickr, quilts, gatherings at the tea party table, cupcakes, craft blogs, Creole tomato sandwiches, her mom's Bernina, and her husband. Peer into her world at handmadecathygaubert.blogspot.com, and do be sure to say "hello."

acknowledgments

Oh my goodness! Can it be possible that this is the most difficult part of the book to write? If that is true (and I think it is!), then it is because there are just so many amazing people who have had a hand (literally and figuratively) in the making of this sweet little book. I am forever thankful: To the amazing group at Lark...what a joy and pleasure it was to make this book with you! To Kathy Sheldon...you gave me a chance (or three?!) that I didn't even know I wanted. To the most marvelous group of designers...you 18 lovely ladies and 1 fabulous fellow have filled the pages of this book with your patchwork goodness. I can never thank you enough for answering my first email with a "yes!" To Jessica VanDerMark...it means so much to me that you captured a little part of our beloved Clotilda for this book. To SueSue Bollinger...you mean the world to me, and it makes me giddy that we are in this together! To Amy Proff Lyons, Angie Tripp, Beki Lambert, Jen Osborn, Theresa Smythe, Verena Carmouche, and family and friends (near and far)...your advice, expertise, and encouragement have been invaluable. To Hillary Lang...yours was one of the first blogs I adored, and your wall of doll quilts captured my heart. Gosh, everything you make captures my heart. You are a constant inspiration! To my parents, DeeDee and Charles Gaubert, and my sisters, Sally and Celie...you are the best of the best, and I am a fortunate daughter and sister indeed. My heart is filled with love and respect for you! To Lily, Eme, and Cate...ah, our lovely, sweet girls! You are the very definition of "triple awesome"!!! You make my heart feel super happy. I am one lucky momma. To Wade, my astoundingly patient husband, without whom this book would surely not exist...there just aren't words enough to thank you for it all, my love! To Amanda Carestio...how on earth did I get so lucky to count you as a friend and editor? Really, at the risk of sounding all "you are the wind beneath my wings"-ish, you truly *are* the wind beneath my wings! To say that I could not have done this without you would be a huge understatement. Simply put, you are absolutely made of awesome. An extra special "thank you" to all of you who make up the ridiculously wondrous community of Flickr (hello, DQS group!) and craft blogs (the writers and the readers). The kindness and support found throughout that incredible place never cease to amaze me!

index

It's all on www.larkcrafts.com

Daily blog posts featuring needlearts, jewelry and beading, and all things crafty

Free, downloadable projects and how-to videos

Calls for artists and book submissions

A free e-newsletter announcing new and exciting books

...and a place to celebrate the creative spirit